Scars that Run Deep

Sometimes the Nightmares Don't End

Patrick Touher

EBURY
PRESS

This edition published 2009 for Index Books Ltd

1 3 5 7 9 10 8 6 4 2

Published in 2008 by Ebury Press, an imprint of Ebury Publishing
A Random House Group Company

This is a revised and updated edition of *Free as a Bird*,
first published in Ireland in 1994

The Random House Group Limited Reg. No. 954009

Addresses for companies within the Random House Group can be found at
www.randomhouse.co.uk

A CIP catalogue record for this book is available from the British Library

The Random House Group Limited supports The Forest Stewardship
Council (FSC), the leading international forest certification organisation. All
our titles that are printed on Greenpeace approved FSC certified paper carry
the FSC logo. Our paper procurement policy can be found at
www.rbooks.co.uk/environment

Printed in the UK by CPI Cox & Wyman, Reading, RG1 8EX

ISBN 9780091925093

To buy books by your favourite authors and register for offers visit
www.rbooks.co.uk

To Paula, John and Suzanne,
May the future be kind to you. A little faith
goes a very long way

*

In grateful thanks to Bishop Dermot O'Mahony
for being there for Pauline

And to Father Michael Carey
for his pastoral care of Paula and Suzanne

Disclaimer

This book is a work of non-fiction based on the experiences and recollections of the author. The names of most characters in the book, including the proper names of the boys in Artane Industrial School, have been changed where necessary to protect privacy. Any resemblance of the substitute names to actual persons is entirely coincidental and unintentional.

Acknowledgements

It is with the greatest of pleasure I get to this part, knowing this book is complete. It's like letting go of a magnificent obsession! I would like to thank the following people for their invaluable help: Colin Guild, my very helpful next-door neighbour, for the huge amount of faxes and emails, and his wife Ellen. My brother-in-law Jim Brennan. I was almost overwhelmed by the encouragement of Jim's wife, Anne. My typist Carine O'Grady. And to Rachel Gordon, April and so many in their office for all the kind help. 'Twas great.

When getting a job done I believe it is the little things that count for so much. I'm so grateful to you all.

My heartfelt thanks to the doctors, nurses and staff of the Medical Centre, Balbriggan for their kind support for Pauline, and to the Irish Motor Neurone Disease Association. To the Eastern Healthboard and Fingal County Council, whose support to Pauline was invaluable.

To all the readers of my last book *Fear of the Collar* for

helping it to become a bestseller in the UK. You all deserve this one. Thank you.

To the staff of Ebury Press: the executive contracts manager James Peak – 'it's as good as it gets', thanks James. To Two Associates, Getty and Alamy for the superb cover design and photographs. To publicist Sarah Townsend. To my editor Justine Taylor for the excellent and expert job you have done editing my huge manuscript. It can't have been an easy task. It flows as it goes now, Justine. For those who have faith and hope and believe in themselves can succeed and achieve their goal. To commissioning editor Charlotte Cole, whose wisdom, vision, faith and belief in my story made this possible. Beholden to you Charlotte.

May the road rise to meet you and fate be kind to you all.

M arch 1958. The day before my sixteenth birthday. The day before I was to leave Artane Industrial Christian Brothers School, the place that had been my home for the past eight years. During those eight years I had suffered many forms of abuse – physical, mental and sexual – and yet what I felt wasn't relief at being free from my tormentors at last, nor was I looking forward to the future; no, what I was experiencing was fear.

I had experienced this emotion many times before, in fact fear engulfed me on a daily basis, but that was the fear of abuse, of being interfered with. What I was going through now was something much less tangible: fear of change.

I was nervous and frightened of having to face a new beginning once again, and to face a world outside, a world so far removed from the one I was leaving behind. The past eight years had been desperately hard and lonely, but at least at Artane I knew what to expect.

Each morning we would march to Mass, and that morning, the one before the day I was to leave, was no different. The sound of marching feet was enormous, a boys' army stamping their hobnail boots loudly down upon the concrete parade ground as though tomorrow would never come. Whenever I think of Artane, that sound comes back to haunt me. The Sheriff's voice echoed from the handball alleys to the church doors: 'Left, left, left right left, lift 'em up or face the wall.'

I wept as the choir sang in Latin at the Mass. In my awful loneliness I had found sanctuary in this beautiful chapel. I found peace and comfort just to sit alone listening to the haunting sounds of the choir as they practised, and as their wonderful sound filled the heavenly air. 'Adoro te Devote' and 'Panis Angelicus' were engraved in my memory.

After Mass I began my last day at work in the bakery. As the last batch of the day was drawn from the two stone ovens I helped Joe Golden, the baker, peel the batch for the final time. Joe winked at me and said, 'Come here, son.' His arm rested around my shoulders, his voice soft. He said, 'Now boys, 'tis time for prayer,' as he said every day. Joe took his baker's flat hat off his bald head. He gazed around at all the boys and said, 'Now let us say a decade of the Rosary for our friend here.' He paused for a moment to look at me, and then continued, 'Patrick leaves us as he came, a friend, but we shall pray to

God that he be kept safe and out of harm's way. As he has no home to go to we pray he finds a nice place to rest. We wish him well, wherever he travels, and we pray that the road rises to meet him. Let us pray. In the name of the Father and of the Son and of the Holy Spirit, let us pray together, boys.'

I felt emotionally drained as I waited for the prayers to end. When they did, old Joe put his flat baker's hat on and led me to the front door. The boys were streaming out of the workshops. 'God be with you, son, all your days,' said Joe. Few men I met in my childhood were worth their salt; Joe Golden was worth his weight in gold.

It was normal finishing time, four o'clock, and we would get to the parade ground between 4 and 4.15 to relax and play games until the Dude, Brother General, blew the whistle for fall in at 4.45pm. Fall in meant every boy had to line up in his division. There were nineteen divisions all lined up for drill exercise given by the drillmaster, who we called Driller the Killer. We marched, slow march and quick march, and marched time, as the Driller, aided by the monitors of each division, shouted, 'Left, left, left right left. Lift 'em up.' In my eight years at Artane the system never changed. At five o'clock we marched to the toilets and out again and then we marched to our classrooms for night school, after which we marched to the chapel at 6.40pm for the Rosary, Benediction and hymns.

After chapel we marched once again in division formation to the refectory for supper. Supper was a loaf of bread between four boys with a bowl of warm dripping to dip bread in and a mug of boiled sweetened tea. Breakfast and supper were always the same, except on Easter Sunday morning when at breakfast each boy received two hard-boiled eggs.

The last day was the same as any other, but as I marched from the refectory I was informed that Brother Shannon – alias Segoogee – wished to see me in the chapel. Segoogee was a quietly spoken, very friendly man. His dog, a red setter, was always by his side. Us boys liked him, and his dog. 'So you are leaving us, boy,' he said to me kindly.

I looked at him, misty eyed, and muttered, 'Yes, sir.'

His smile widened as he held out a piece of paper to me. 'Here, boy, take it. You will go to work for this man in Fairview.'

I remember that the organist was playing all the while I was in the sacristy of the beautiful old chapel. The Latin hymn 'Pange Lingua' filled the air scented with the blessed incense after the evening Benediction. I left Segoogee, the piece of paper unopened, feeling more confused and depressed than ever. As I made my way to my dormitory for the last time, a strange feeling came over me. Tomorrow I'll be free, I thought, and smiled to myself.

I entered the dormitory as the Sheriff was beating the kids who were facing the wall. His stern voice rang loud and clear.

'Brogan, you pup, playing soccer. You know it is an English game and strictly forbidden, yet you defy us and insist on breaking the rules. Bend over that bed, lift up your night-shirt, this will teach you to obey. You will suffer for the poor souls in Purgatory.' The sound of the leather crashing against naked flesh made my body crawl. Each stroke brought another terrifying scream and shouts from the terrified child. 'Please, oh please, sir, I won't play soccer again I promise, sir. Please, sir, you're killing me.'

The Sheriff's response was loud and crystal clear. 'I know you won't, boy, because I will crucify you, you pup.'

I got into my bed that night as terrified as any night in the previous eight years, all the fears of my childhood haunting me.

That last night of my eight years at Artane was just like any other gone before. In my dreams I was being hounded by men in black chasing after me over the hills with guns. I screamed and screamed for help as they drew closer and closer to me as I came to the cliff's edge. Looking down I was terrified and screamed.

When I woke up I was outside on the parade ground in the freezing cold, dressed only in my night-shirt. I had been walking in my sleep again. Arms were around me, a voice spoke softly in my ear. 'You've been sleepwalking, come back with me now, son.'

I was safe in the arms of Angel Face. I felt good.

'What time is it, sir?' I asked.

'It's almost 4am, boy. Time you got some real sleep.'

When I woke up it was my sixteenth birthday. I was awakened, as usual, by the voice of the Sheriff shouting, 'Up, up, up, you pups, first three rows into wash, last two in face the wall.' It was the day I was to leave Artane, the day I had to stand on my own two feet, to work for my keep in a world far removed from what I had been used to for the last eight years.

As I made my bed to perfection I felt a twinge of sadness. I glanced up and there I could see my pal Rasher, his towel at the ready. He winked at me. I nodded over to Quickfart, who smiled and pretended to look busy while we waited for our turn to go into the washroom.

There were long rows of white wash-hand basins. A rack on the wall held the toothbrushes, and I shared mine with a lot of other boys. I dived on a red lump of carbolic soap and scrubbed my hands and face; then I scrubbed my teeth with the same soap and handed my brush to Quickfart. He was delighted. 'Thanks, Collie, you're a pal.'

Rasher shouted, 'Can I have it after yeh, Quickfart? I don't aim to be last out. The feckin' Sheriff is on, yeh know.'

I paused for a moment to look out the tall windows of the washroom, facing south. I got a glimpse of the outside world

– Marino, Donnycarney, and beyond. I'd be out there within a few hours. But instead of anticipation, I was dreading my departure; I was not used to change and it terrified me.

My thoughts were broken by the Sheriff screaming, 'Last two out will face the wall! You'll suffer for the poor souls in Limbo, I promise!'

Poor Blossom and the Skunk were the last out, and the Sheriff wasted no time in dealing with them. 'Last again, Blossom! You'll have to learn to hurry yourself up. Bend down, touch your toes, boy. Remember the poor souls in Purgatory and Limbo.' He gave him six of the best then he told the Skunk to bend over. The lad was a tough sort; he refused. The Sheriff grabbed hold of him and forced him over the nearest bed a few feet away and flogged the backside off him, to the sounds of 'Leave me alone, leave me alone, you swine!'

That morning, as the boys' choir sang the Latin hymns, I wept openly. I was a Christian Brothers' boy through and through, and after such a long period in their care I had become institutionalised. Even though I lived in a state of fear for most of my days at Artane, it was preferable to the unknown terrors of the world outside its gates. At that moment, if someone had offered me the chance to stay, even though it would mean continuing with the abuse I had undergone over the past eight years, I would have grabbed it with both hands. When I glanced up I saw the Sheriff singing with all the strength of his conviction. I knew he was a dedicated man, like so many of his colleagues. But for all that conviction he had such an evil streak in him. Even as a child of just ten years old I had experienced the violent, sadistic nature of this tall, fearsome Christian Brother.

As we filed out I was stopped by Brother Monaghan, who smiled and took my hand in his. He spoke softly. 'Take good care now, and remember us in your prayers, Collie. Go to Mass and visit the house of God often.' His last words almost had me in tears. 'I hope we were not too hard on you, Collie.'

I stumbled out of the church.

I quickly joined up with my division. The monitor came towards me, smiled and said, 'Last day, Collie! Soon you'll be free of all this.' Then the Macker blew his whistle for us to march off to the refectory for the first meal of the day.

As the last of the fifteen divisions marched up the centre passage to chants of 'Left, left, left right left', I felt tears in my eyes. I had no thirst or hunger for food or drink, as my thoughts were elsewhere.

The Drisco approached me and spoke quickly. 'You're leaving after all these years. How are you going to manage without us?' I wondered that too. As I was about to say, 'I don't know,' he reached out his fat hand to say goodbye. I just cried.

The Drisco was a tough, hard Brother, short, stocky and with a fierce temper on him; a difficult man to get to know. As a boy working in the kitchens, I feared but never totally disliked him. When he was in a bad mood he was dangerous, like a mad bull. There were times when he punched the head off me or beat me with a long, heavy stick for some silly thing that went wrong in the kitchen, forgetting to put the sugar in the tea boiler, perhaps, or leaving out the salt in the soup – yet when he was being nice, he was likeable. He was an odd sort of character. As he gripped my hand I could tell he was being sincere. 'Have you a home to go to now when you get out?'

I said, 'No, sir. I don't know where I'm going, sir.' I hadn't yet had the courage to look at Segoogee's instructions.

Suddenly the Sheriff blew his whistle for grace after meals, and the Drisco boomed out in his clear Cork accent, 'Good luck now, and may God be with you. I'll say the Rosary for you; and you'll go to Mass and say your prayers now.'

The Sheriff's whistle sounded for march-out. The monitors shouted, 'By the left, quick march! Left, left, left right left! Lift them up or face the wall!' I glanced behind me and caught sight of the Sheriff for the last time as he clattered a boy across the face so hard that he was knocked to the floor.

Some things just never change, I thought, as I marched to the parade ground. I had as much fear as ever in me as I swung my arms high and stamped my hobnailed boots as hard as I could, even knowing it was the last time I would have to go through it. I was glad when the monitor shouted, 'Halt! At ease! Fall out!'

I was tense and emotional as I stood before the Macker, who was standing with the drillmaster on parade. They smiled, shook my hand and wished me well. As I marched up to the storeroom to collect my new suit and working clothes for my life outside, thoughts of my first day back in 1950 flooded my mind – it was here I had come to when I received my first Artane clothes and hobnailed boots.

After saying goodbye to my pals and a few Brothers I encountered, I was on my way out of one of the toughest institutions in Ireland, yet I found it hard to hold back the tears.

I put my hand into my pocket to take out the address Segoogee had given me earlier. He said they would put me up and I would be at home there – but I could have kicked him! The writing was just a scribble. I couldn't make out the home I was to go to, or indeed the address of the bakery I was to work in either.

It was a long walk from the parade ground to the bus stop on the Malahide Road. I felt utterly alone. A car approached as I passed the old quarry to my right. I noticed two young lads aged about twelve years old in the back. The driver shouted, 'Could you tell me the way to the main office?'

'Yes, sir, you'll find it on your right, just as you pass the statue of the Sacred Heart.'

I glanced at the two boys seated in the back and I couldn't help it – the tears flowed down my cheeks. I hurried across the Malahide Road and waited anxiously for the bus that would bring me into the future.

2

Although I entered Artane Industrial School just before my eighth birthday, I remember my life before then well, and with great fondness. Mr and Mrs Doyle, my foster parents, treated me with kindness, and their children Margaret, Edward and John were like sister and brothers to me. We lived in a small, whitewashed cottage in the hills of Barnacullia, past Sandyford, County Dublin. The little cottage had just two rooms and a pantry. How and where we all slept – the Doyle family, five in all, with me making six – I cannot quite remember; yet we were comfortable and happy.

Back then, in those days, I can't recall ever being so much as slapped. I had no fears of anything or anyone, not even of the dark. Life was so carefree then. I often walked home from school with my pals through the fields and across the hillside to Carthy's Green, where they'd help me bring in the cows with Margaret Doyle. Margaret taught me how to milk the cows; one of them – the oldest cow – was nicknamed Big Betty. A great cow was Betty. Shep the collie dog followed Margaret and me everywhere over across the hills to bring in the cows. And every morning Shep would follow me down the dirt track to as far as the Tiller Doyle's shop. A real pal was Shep.

We had no running water or electricity in them days up in Barnacullia, not that I recall, though we were all happy then. Bridget Doyle, my foster mother, baked our bread, scones and apple pies. Every day after school it was my job to fetch buckets of clear water from the well along the hillside.

Even though I was not related to the Doyles, I was treated just like a member of their family. In fact, after I left Artane, I was never once interested to find out who my father was, or even if he was still alive. As far as I was concerned, even back then in 1958, any man worth his salt would never desert his own flesh and blood, so I couldn't care less about him. All I knew of my mother, Helen, was that she died when I was very young. When she became too ill to take care of me she left me with the nuns in St Brigid's Convent, Eccles Street, Dublin, opposite the Mater Hospital. I was just twelve months old.

In my later years I would be plagued by nightmares, but as a child I can't recall ever experiencing bad dreams. My dreams were pleasant, happy ones, just like my days living up on the hillside of Barnacullia.

Memories of Barnacullia

From the clear mountain streams

In the hearts of my dreams

To the beauty that surrounds Barnacullia.

Of my fond childhood days

Through the sun's twilight rays

In my thoughts, you should know I am with ya!

My childhood dreams like visions to me

Of sunlit waters and children carefree

From the Doyle's cottage door

My vision so clear

Barnacullia to Sandyford and the road to Glencullen

I walked without fear.

The cottage of my dreams, I see visions

Of Bridget, Roseanna and John

As I gaze through the window with sadness

No light in the heart – 'tis gone

Fond memories of Barnacullia, inscribed so tenderly

As I remember young Margaret.

As a wee orphan, she cared for me.

I was in foster care from November 1942, when I was one, until just before my eighth birthday in March 1950. No one that I know of ever came to me and explained much about why I was an orphan living in such a picturesque home. It was never explained to me who I *really* was, I was not even sure of my actual birthday or my real name. To this day no one ever bothered to explain to me the reasons for my arrest from the cottage, and driven away by the police in a big black Ford estate car to a courthouse, and stood before a judge at 10am on a cold, bright, spring morning. In fact the judge didn't even tell me I was to serve the remainder of my childhood in the incredibly brutal notorious Artane Industrial School, run by the Christian Brothers. However, I learned in due course that I was not alone in my grim mysterious world. At least five of my best school pals from Barnacullia were to join me within a year of my arrival. Although they had real parents, they had been in foster care as I had.

I will always remember my arrival in Artane. I was in the main office. Outside the sky was an unbroken shade of blue. The boys were at work on the flowerbeds as I stood at the long pull-up window staring out at them.

I didn't worry about how awful the boy gardeners looked in their awful drab serge tufted clothes. I believed the judge in the Court House in Kilmainham when he said I'd be only away for a few weeks.

As I enjoyed the plateful of fruit cake one Brother gave to me, I had no reason to be afraid, or to fear these nice Brothers dressed in long black cassocks. To me at that time I thought

they were all saints, just like the one who gave me the cake –
the very old Brother who, I was soon to learn, was nicknamed
the Saint.

I waited, as I had been told to by the Saint, for the clerk of
the office to come out to see me. When the brown-panelled
office door opened, I looked towards the tall young office
clerk. 'Here, take this and remember it. It's your serial
number, boy. It will stay with you until you are released,' he
said. 'It's stamped on your boots and shoes, suits and day
clothes.' He smiled at me as he handed me the dog tag with
my serial number. I glanced down at it in amazement. It read
No. 12928. 'You won't forget it will you.' His smile was warm
and sincere.

'No sir.' But I'm only here for a few weeks I thought as he
returned to his office.

As I look back to that moment on a beautiful spring
morning in March 1950 I never once realised that this would
be my number until my release on reaching the age of sixteen,
a full eight awful years, half of my childhood locked up
as number 12928 in Artane Industrial School. My childhood as
I had known it was gone for ever, yet no one had the courage
or decency to tell me.

Some tunes will always linger or remain in the back of one's
mind. A tune that when you hear it, no matter where you are,
will remind you of the time and place you were in when first

you heard it. As I was being led down the granite stone steps by the monitor to meet the Dude, the Brother General, 'The Foggy Dew' swept the grounds of this mighty Christian Brothers boys' industrial school. 'What's that?' I said.

The monitor, whose name was Billy, smiled as he explained, 'That's our famous boys' band. They're playing "The Foggy Dew". They're practising for the St Patrick's Day Grand Parade. Come on, follow me. You've got to meet the Dude.'

Sure, I couldn't quite take it all in as Billy seemed to be so excited, explaining all these things to me. But then I was very slow on learning, on the uptake of things. However, I had a mind that stored up what I'd seen, heard and had done to me, and I'd never be allowed to forget such things!

As the hauntingly beautiful sound of 'The Foggy Dew' swept through the air, the boys' parade ground, where 900 boys were lined up in their respective divisions, looked like a mighty boys' army. I was shocked at the awesome sight. 'What are they doing?' I asked.

Billy quickly explained, 'The boys are lined up in their divisions. Each division goes by age, see.' He pointed. 'Look, there, that's Division One, they're the older boys, fifteen years of age and over. At sixteen they are set free. You will be in a division called the nineteenth, as you are the youngest. Now you've got to meet the Great Brother General.'

'Who's he?' I said, scared, confused and bewildered.

'He's the Dude, Pat. He's the General Brother in charge. He likes good kids, so you'll be okay.'

Suddenly a thundering sound, like a drum roll; the beat carried like a huge echo. 'What's that?' I said, looking at Billy. I reached for his hand. Relief swept through me as he clenched it in his. 'That's our boys' band playing "The Minstrel Boy", it's a famous march. We hold our own parades here. Every division marches in it, and the boys' parents are allowed to attend all parades for great occasions such as St Patrick's Day, Easter Sunday and Corpus Christi, which are the school's biggest and best. When you're older, you will get to march with your own division.'

'Gosh, really,' I shouted over the music. 'I'd only ever followed our local band from our school in Sandyford to over yonder in Stepaside.'

Billy gasped, pulled me to one side and said, 'I want you to forget words like gosh, and over yonder, as it's far too posh for us in here!'

Suddenly, I felt change sweeping in over me, change I'd never believe I'd get used to; change was a word I grew to hate. As the monitor explained angrily to me, 'Look Pat, you got to change, your choice of words will bring nothing but trouble to you. The kids here will make shit ou-ra-yeh, *over bleedin' yonder*, are you kidding me, Pat? Even the kids in your nineteenth will laugh their heads off at yeh.' His tone softened as he continued. 'Look at me. I want you to listen to me. This is a very tough place for a kid as young as you. But being so young without any folks won't get you special privileges. Believe me, this is a very unforgiving place. There is no room for posh, fancy words, Pat. In here, we got our own slang words for most things so I'm asking you to change. It's not for the best but it's for your own good. You drop your fancy expressions such as "over yonder", and "oh, gosh", do you understand?'

I nodded, a silent, frightened yes. I began to hate him as I felt so scared.

'Look, Pat. They call me The Sly. It's my nickname, okay? You'll have one by the end of the week. Now watch me carefully, Pat!'

As I was very slow on grasping things, and on the uptake, it would take a long time for me to realise I'd never again be allowed to return to my cottage home, to a normal life in the hills of south County Dublin in Barnacullia.

Billy was right, of course. As a monitor he knew the ropes. Nothing would ever be so normal again, not in my childhood. I was only just eight years of age, and I had been thrust into Artane Industrial School, just one in an army of 900. The scars run deep.

I was no longer the child with the blushing smile from the hillside cottage home in beautiful picturesque Barnacullia. I became hardened and Artane slang words took over from my way of expressing myself.

My pleasant boyhood dreams of clear-water streams, plush pastures green, of the hills, and my pals, and going to school through fields, and growing up in a normal life in a cottage home all began to fade. As my dreams slowly became darker I began to walk in my sleep. My dreams turned to nightmares as I fought my demons. I was hunted and haunted as I ran from men in black.

New visions haunted my dreams. Boys wet their beds through fear, fear of the collar; fear of the men in black. I wet my bed on just a few occasions in the early years, 1950 to 1952. I remember one bitter cold morning in the winter of 1951. The Brothers known as the Apeman and the Sheriff were on duty. After wash-up time we knelt down for morning prayers by our well-made beds. The Apeman marched up and down the long centre passage. The Sheriff stood in front of the altar and said the prayers, which we repeated together out loud. At the end he said, 'Remember what Christ Our Lord Jesus said, "Little Children come unto me". Remember in your prayers the good the Christian Brothers do for you.'

'Pray for us,' we repeated aloud.

Then he said, 'Any boy who soiled or wet their bed, report

to the monitor and bring your soiled and wet sheets with you as we leave. Boys with dirty sheets must march around the centre lamp on the parade until all the boys are in the chapel. Boys with wet or soiled bedclothes must then march to the laundry and hand in your dirty linen.'

That freezing cold morning I was one of the kids who'd wet the bed. I marched around the tall lamp post in the snow and ice. I had no overcoat, or gloves, as I recall. I cried with the pain of the cold as my fingers ached. I remember that, as I marched in a circle with a dozen boys, the Brother on parade duty was dressed in his long black cassock and a cloak was draped round his broad shoulders, his hat down over his forehead to keep the snow from his eyes. The Dude's voice rang out crisp and as ice cold as the bitter east wind, 'Left, left, left right left, lift 'em up or face the wall.'

That wall haunted my dreams. We were made to stand there with our hands held high straight above our heads. It was torture. On bitter cold winter mornings no mercy was shown or given to those of us who were told to face the wall. We would face the wall just for being the last two or three in or out of the freezing cold wash room. And as we stood there, we'd be beaten across our naked bottoms, six of the best from the Apeman or the Sheriff with their iron-hard leathers. The pain was more cruel and excruciating as a result of the cold.

In the autumn of 1952, late in the afternoon, I was playing

with my pals the Burner, Oxo, Minnie, Stewie, Jamjar and Bubbles. We were playing conkers when Bubbles threw one at Jamjar. The chestnut missed its intended target and hit the Brother known as Hellfire in the face. It was around five, an hour before night school, as I recall.

The Brother came over to us. He was clutching the handle of a hurley stick. 'Hands up the boy who threw the large chestnut at me.'

I stood back as I feared this evil man.

Bubbles went forward. 'It was me, sir. I'm sorry sir. It was an accident sir.'

The Hellfire's voice rose. 'Good. I like honesty. Now I will put the smirk where your pals can't see it. Trousers down, you pup. Touch your toes. Now one stroke for every day in the year, to set an example to other brats like you.'

I counted silently as the Brother wielded the stick across the boy's buttocks 365 times. The Hellfire paused to wipe the sweat from his flushed face when he had completed the horrendous beating. Bubbles was lying in a heap on the ground, his body shivering beneath the gold of the late October sun. The Hellfire looked at me and my pals and said, 'Take him down to the Infirmary. Let the nurse take care of him then get back in time for class.'

My nightmares were formed out of such awful moments. My nightmares and sleepwalking and shouting in my sleep came about as a direct result of the constant brutal beatings I experienced, and from witnessing other boys in my class and in the same dormitory receiving the same violent attacks.

But there were other forms of abuse, too. I first experienced sexual abuse as early as the autumn of 1950. My dreams began to darken as a direct result of the hard core of Christian Brothers who enjoyed beating boys, naked, black and blue for minor trivial offences, physical and sexual abuse of boys in their care.

I had been torn away from a normal life in the loving bosom of a family home in the hillside in Barnacullia, and that scarred me. And Artane scarred me, it shattered my hopes and dreams. These scars are deeply engraved in my memory, in my heart and in my soul.

I was in my first year. I was in dormitory five, it was mid-November, an awful windy night. Since then I have always dreaded the month of November, always have done since.

The Macker and the Bucko were two tall men. We all feared them as they could be so cruel, even inside the classrooms.

That evening I awoke to find the Macker standing by my bedside. His voice was huskily deep. He'd scared me as he pulled the bedclothes down, pulled up my night-shirt to reveal my nakedness. His foul breath smelt of tobacco.

I've never ever forgotten his first words. 'Why are you sleeping on your tummy?'

At that moment I was so frightened, so alone and in fear. Not just of the November storms but because I had no one to cry out to for help. When the Macker spoke again I cried out, 'I want to go home, sir. Please, sir.'

He leaned in over me and smiled, 'Yes, now why were you lying on your tummy, boy?'

'I don't know, sir. I don't understand, sir,' I half muttered, unaware what was on his mind or why he was asking such a question. It was then the very tall, very strict Brother arrived, known as the Bucko. Most kids called them the Terrible Twins. Two dark, evil men.

The Macker put his hand on my penis. I was shocked and I felt really awful as now there were two of them. 'What's this for, boy? Tell me no lies.' The Macker held my penis. The Bucko leaned in over me. His voice was low, his breath was stale, and made me feel sick. I've hated the stale smell of tobacco ever since.

'I don't know, sir. I don't understand, sir. Honest, sir.' I felt so scared. I was terrified of them both. 'I don't know, sir.'

The Macker kept feeling my penis. It hurt. 'The truth, boy, or I will scourge you naked.' How I cried; I wanted desperately to scream.

'What is this for, you pup?' The Bucko's words made me

shiver while the Macker felt me, his finger forced up into my anus. I just wept.

The Macker forced down my foreskin with his thumb, all the while feeling and holding my small penis and testicles. I just cried out, 'I don't know, sir. Honest, sir.' The Macker's smoky breath fanned my lips as he leaned over me. I blurted, 'I pass water with it sir.' I waited, stark naked, and too scared to move a muscle.

'Are you sure that's all it's for, boy?' said the Bucko. 'No lies now, or I will trounce you naked, you pup.'

The Macker pulled down my night-shirt as he said, 'Tell me, boy, what's it for and why you lie on your stomach, or I will have you in my room.'

'I go to the toilet, sir, to pass water, sir. I often sleep flat on my tummy, sir, as I feel good, sir, it's comfortable, sir.'

'So you feel real good, boy, lying flat on your stomach, and you talk in your sleep, boy. Tell me who Big Betty is, you filthy pup. You talk dirty in your sleep boy.' I stared at the Macker. There was a weird grin on his face. His voice was deep, husky, very low and frightening. 'The truth, boy, or I will scourge you, I mean it.'

I knew both of them meant it.

'She's an old cow, sir, my favourite cow, sir.'

The Brothers just laughed. 'A cow. Big Betty is a cow?' said the Macker.

'Yes, sir, it's true, sir. I helped Maggie milk her every day, after school.'

I hated those two Christian Brothers, who haunted my dreams and helped to destroy my childhood. That was the first sexual encounter I had as a child.

After they left me I turned over to lie flat on my tummy when I suddenly remembered the words from the Macker and the Bucko. 'You'll commit sin, boy, lying flat on your tummy.' So I lay on my side, my eyes wide open. I tried to sleep. I closed my eyes when suddenly I heard the hauntingly beautiful sound of 'The Four Green Fields' filling the spacious dormitory. As most of the boys slept I lay awake listening.

'Yeh still awake, Collie?' whispered my friend the Burner.

'Yes, I can't sleep,' I said. 'My thing hurts me.'

'I know, you had a shagging nightmare. Now here comes the bleedin' Whistler.'

'But he's okay. I like him, although he scares me.'

'A bleedin' shadow scares the bleedin shit ou-ra-yeh Collie. I know 'cos they were feeling you up and messing about with yeh, cos you're a good-looking kid and an orphan. They'll bleedin' have you, Collie.'

I closed my eyes and listened to the beautiful haunting sound of 'The Four Green Fields'. The Whistler was a tall, middle-aged Christian Brother, a gentle giant. I wished to

God all Christian Brothers could be like the Whistler but I guess it was just wishful thinking. He was unique and he was very well liked and respected. In my time I had never seen him use physical force or use the hard leather. He cut a daunting figure as he patrolled up the dormitory after lights out. Often he'd linger at the rear of the dormitory and in the long dark corridors whistling 'The Foggy Dew' or 'The Four Green Fields'. The sound would echo through the dormitories like he was telling us he was there. This gave me hope. I guess that's what made him so special.

In Artane Industrial School I kept all of my very worst experiences a closely guarded secret. I feared speaking of such awful embarrassing things, and I never understood them or, in my own naive and gullible way, did I ever really comprehend or realise the depth of satisfaction men like the Macker got from the power they wielded over us in such a brutal, physical way.

Looking back at what I experienced and witnessed, much of the physical abuse, and the way in which the worst of the Christian Brothers inflicted pain and punishment, was to a large extent sexually motivated. Young orphan boys like me bore the brunt of this physical and sexual torture. I remember so clearly how fearful the hours between prayer and sleep were. It was the night sounds. As I tried to sleep they became a big part of my nightmares.

3

It took almost two years for me to become a hardened Artaner, and I was glad when my tenth birthday came around in March 1952: not because of birthday presents or a birthday cake and cards – there were no such luxuries in Artane – but because I was to report to the Brother in charge after breakfast to be given a job. I was to be placed in a new division and a new dormitory and, best of all, I was now allowed to take part in parades and the Corpus Christi processions.

I got up that morning as usual at half past six, while the Brother on duty, the Apeman, stood in the centre passage shouting, 'Up, up, you pups! First three rows out to wash. Last two out will face the wall. Bed-wetters report to the monitor at the double. Soilers bring their soiled sheets to the boot room. I'll make you suffer for the poor souls in Purgatory, you filthy wretches! Next three rows out to wash on the double. Last two back will face the wall!'

Though it was my birthday, it was just like any previous morning in Artane. Whether it was your birthday or Christmas Day or if there was four feet of snow outside, the regimental system remained the same. Break the rules of silence in dormitory, chapel, toilets or classroom and you were put out to face the wall or, when on parade, sent to the charge room to face the Dude or Driller the Killer.

That morning in 1952 I took my place in my old division, the sixteenth. I had a good feeling about the day ahead. When the Brother in charge shouted, 'By the left, quick march!' I glanced to my right at Quickfart and said, 'Thank heavens this is our last day in this division.'

'Yeah, I hear they're lookin' for five or six new boys for the refectory. The Brother in charge is a madman.'

'What's his name?'

'The Drisco.'

Suddenly I was scared of a man I had never met. At Mass I prayed the Dude would send me to the Sewing Room in the Long Hall. But my prayers were not answered. I was sent to work in the boys' refectory, seven days a week, until I was fourteen.

I will never forget the noise at mealtimes in the refectory. As soon as the Brother on duty blew his whistle for us to begin to eat we had to shout over each other to be heard, and we had to defend what we were given from other hungry boys.

As a hardened Artaner I enjoyed a good punch-up, and mealtimes were looked upon as 'mill' time, when fights often broke out over trivial things such as the loaf of bread not being divided evenly.

It had taken all of those first two years for me to adjust to the strict military system. In those early days I lay awake for hours at night listening to other lads crying. They had different reasons for their tears. Some of them were bed-wetters who were flogged in the boot room before going to bed – flogged not just for dirtying the bedclothes but also for being too slow to report it or not reporting it at all. I was one of those who believed the story that our dormitory was haunted by the Devil and that he promised he would return some night to scorch the building. In the early 1960s, in fact, it came about. My old dormitory, along with the cinema, was burned to the ground.

My worst fears, however, were reserved for the classroom. I feared the hard men like the Hellfire, the Lug, the Bucko, the Macker and the Sheriff. But in class I was known as a duffer, and I was awful at spelling, writing and maths. My poor backside was always on fire from the pain of the hard leather.

I had been sentenced to eight years in Artane Industrial School for being an orphan. What a crime! But I was not alone in that valley of tears, as so many others cried for their mothers' love, only to be told to shut up by the Hellfire or the Apeman. I found sanctuary in the chapel, and I often stole away from the gang to be alone on cold, wet days in winter. I became emotional at the singing of the Latin Mass, and often wept as the boys' choir sang the beautiful Latin hymns. I escaped, too, in my dreams. I walked the road from Barnacullia to the old schoolhouse in Sandyford a thousand times as I dreamed of my stolen childhood. It took many years for me to realise that there'd be no going back. In reality it was now only a beautiful dream.

When I first entered Brother Paul's class in the autumn of 1952 I was not alone in feeling the bitter wind of change. From the moment he stood before us, I instantly felt terrified of the man nicknamed the Sheriff. I may have been naive and gullible, but I was nobody's fool. I could rebel at any given time, particularly when I was getting a severe beating for a mere triviality, only to lead myself into further trouble and to find myself placed on a two-week charge, to stand guard on some bloody gate during recreation times and to prevent boys from escaping. Fat chance I had of ever preventing a kid from escape as I was very small and I so desperately wanted to run away myself many times.

Every Christian Brother was issued with a long leather, about eighteen inches in length, two inches wide and half an inch thick. These long, hard leathers were made several lengths of leather put together. Inserted in the lower half were slats of lead or iron to add weight and pain. The strips were then sewn together in the bootmakers' workshop on the machines.

The Brothers used these long, painful leathers inside the classrooms for even the most minor of offences, such as getting sums and spellings incorrect, and most of the Christian Brothers used the leathers with force and brutality. Boys who were ordered at any given time to face the wall would receive six to twelve strokes across the hands or buttocks. When used with brute force against naked flesh, the pain was quite simply excruciating. I suffered horrendous pain from beatings I received from the Brothers in the classrooms on a regular basis.

The Sheriff had an uncontrollable vicious streak in him. For many years I was in his class and in his dormitory; both were run with fear through brutal physical force. I was often brutally attacked by this man, as were so many kids, for bad spelling, for bad grammar or for quite simply getting some question he'd asked me wrong. Even his tone had a cutting edge to it.

On one particular occasion in 1953 he indicated that I should come to the top of the class. I was so frightened of this brutal man, who so often whipped boys across the face and head with his open hands that I was just too scared to stand close to him. I always tried to stand back, but that day he was determined to get his evil way. 'Move closer to me, boy, so I can get a clear view of you,' he ordered. As I moved in closer I could smell his foul tobacco-tainted breath.

The first smack landed on the right side of my jaw. As I raised my hand to feel it, the second smack landed over my left ear and knocked me to the floor. Bells were ringing out inside my throbbing head as he pounded my face, both sides with fierce blows. I had witnessed him beat many of my pals in the classroom in similar fashion. As I licked the blood from my lips a thumping dull sound, similar to the fierce thundering sound of marching feet, swept the classroom as the Sheriff physically pulled me up by the hair from the floor. The noise grew louder and louder, and I dimly became aware that the entire class was chanting, 'We want out, we want out, why are we waiting for the big break-out?' The Sheriff stared down at my bloodied face, his voice filled with hate. 'Face the wall, hold your hands straight above your head, drop 'em, you pup, and I will flog you naked.'

While I stood that morning facing the wall as I was ordered to, the Sheriff suddenly drew out his long hard leather and attacked the boys, brutally beating them across the head and face, while shouting at them to be quiet. When the classroom fell silent he ordered every kid in the class to bend over the desks and he systematically flogged every boy across the buttocks.

To this day I blame the Christian Brothers who used physical violence in the classrooms to get results, such as the Sheriff, the Macker, the Hellfire and many like them, for depriving me of getting a decent education. I feared entering their classrooms so much I couldn't spell my own name. These men were men of violence who used fear to gain complete control over us. Boys wet their beds at night as they slept, soaked in fear of these evil, brutal men who were nothing more than a band of sadists and a discredit to the order of the Christian Brothers.

It was mostly the same teak-tough band of Brothers such as the Hellfire, The Apeman, the Bucko, the Macker, the Lug, the Sheriff, the Drisco and Joey Boy who acted out and performed their acts of cruelty on a regular basis. They went about the task of physically and sexually abusing boys under their evil control with a certain degree of lustful satisfaction and ultimate power. On any given day this cruel gang of Brothers dished out whatever form of punishment for any mere trivial offence to those boys who were ordered to face the wall. The punishment would depend on the mood these Christian Brothers were in once they were on duty.

When the Sheriff, the Macker and the drill instructor, Driller the Killer, were on duty together they were a frightening evil force. While in command of the Saturday showers and on general duty in charge over all the boys on parade during recreation, they were in their element.

Whenever I look back to the worst moments I experienced, I think of the brutality I witnessed at close quarters in that shower room in my early years, 1950 to 1955. These memories are among the hardest to bear.

As a ten-year-old I suffered at the cruel hands of the Macker and Hellfire, the Sheriff and Driller the Killer inside the shower room. I felt degraded and quite often humiliated at having to march naked in my division up the long back hall to enter the shower.

I remember one particular Saturday back in February 1952. As I lined up on the snow- and ice-covered parade ground in the fifteenth division, a bitter cold wind swept over us. The vast grounds were white. I felt pangs of hunger, even though I'd just had my slice of thick bread which was dipped in hot dripping and a mug of tea!

The Dude stood on the wooden platform dressed in his long black cloak, his black hat dipped to shade his eyes from the snow. He was built like an American quarterback. Alongside of him stood the most fearsome drill instructor: Driller the Killer. A monitor took charge of each division. Billy the Sly was in charge of ours.

Quickfart whispered as he covered his mouth with his

hand, yet his words were picked up. 'Hey, Collie. The Dude, he's like a bleedin gangster, Harry Lime, remember in *The Third Man*.' I nodded a silent yes as the monitor came close to us.

This monitor would have got on well in the Hitler youth movement, I thought.

His voice rose above the Dude's, pointing at Quickfart, then at me. 'Face the wall inside the shower room. You will suffer for breaking the rules.'

Just then a packed hard snowball crashed against the monitor's head. I watched him grasp his face as he went down on his knees, covering his eyes. I heard a voice. 'Ou-ra the bleedin' way, Collie.' The Burner put the first kick in, followed by Stewie and Quickfart. The Sly was pelted with snowballs before help arrived.

On hard, cold days in the depths of winter, when the snow fell, boys took their revenge on monitors and Brothers alike. No monitor was well liked.

That Saturday I marched with my division from the snow-covered grounds to the back hall. As the voice of the Dude rang out, 'Left, left, left right left,' I wondered who was on duty inside the shower room, hoping it was not the Macker.

The monitor shouted, 'Division get ready. Halt. Stand at ease. Take your clothes off. Fold them up neatly and form up in silence.'

I lined up naked behind the Burner. 'Who's on duty?'

Whispering swept through the long hall when the big doors opened wide. The Macker, Hellfire and the Sheriff could be seen with Driller the Killer. I felt scared. What a team, I thought to myself. Then the order was given, 'Division. Attention. Division by the left, quick march. No talking. Every boy must get soap and brush. Left, left, left right left.'

I marched with my naked division of sixty boys with fear in my heart. Fear so many of us shared as we marched into the spacious shower room. The air filled with steam. As I stood facing the tiled wall, as I had been ordered to do by the monitor, the Macker's voice rang out, 'Any boy without soap or brush face the wall. Hands straight above your heads.' I could taste his smoke-tainted breath as he stood close to me. Then I heard the sound of leather crashing off naked buttocks mixed with screams of terror.

I dropped my arms aching with pain for a few satisfying moments of utter relief. But to my horror I was caught. I knew the voice. His smell. It was the Macker. 'Oh God, help me,' I murmured as my name was called. My naked body froze with fear.

'Did you shower, boy?'

Afraid to look up at him I could hear Quickfart shouting at Hellfire, 'Leave me alone, yeh bleedin' evil bastard.' His screams filled me with fear. 'Bend down. Spread your legs wide, boy.' The Macker's voice was low and deep. 'You lied, you pup, you lied.'

'No, sir, no sir. Honest, sir.

'Your anus is filthy, you did not scrub your anus, boy. Did you?'

'I don't understand you, sir. Honest, sir.'

'There's so much you don't understand, boy. If you don't know where your anus is, then I will show you.' Suddenly I was lifted off my feet. I felt a lump of soap being forced up my back passage. I cried out but it was in vain. As he raised his voice, 'I will scrub your anus for you, boy,' I felt him push the broken half of a broom handle up inside me. As he withdrew it, I cried out. His voice was severe now. 'This is for telling me lies, boy. Bend over, hands touching your toes, boy.' The pain was excruciating as the leather crashed off my wet naked buttocks.

Then Driller the Killer blew the whistle for us to leave the showers and get towelled off. I felt relief as I dried myself down. Except for the awful stinging pain up my back passage, I'll be okay, I thought.

I marched out of the shower room with my division to get dressed. Just as a division of older boys marched past us I got a glimpse of Oxo and the Burner. As I got dressed, murmuring swept over our division. 'There's a mill, there's a big bleedin' big mill. Look,' said Stewie, 'it's Driller the Killer and two farm hands.'

I followed the kids to look on as two tough farm hands wrestled Driller the Killer to the ground. The Driller took a real beating from a few of the older boys before order was restored. I watched with many lads from my division as one of the farm hands was carried out and down to the Infirmary. Later we learned the boy received a broken arm and a busted nose for his troubles.

As I recall these incidents, I remember saying to my pal Minnie, 'Can it get any worse here?' He laughed as usual at being asked a question. I remember how he looked at me that day out on the snow-covered parade ground. He said, 'I'm in here just as you are. But I hope it does, cos I love watching a good mill. So do you.'

For the most part, the vast majority of the Christian Brothers were of good stock. There were good men who were not so hard or cruel to us kids in care. Many of these Christian Brothers used their free time to help and participate in sporting activities with us. Some of them organised drama and worked the projector on the cinema on Saturdays. They were hard when they had to be, but never cruel, evil or sadistic. Most were good men and true to us and to their order.

But then there were the rest. The child molesters, like Joey Boy and the Macker. As in all walks of life, there are those perverted men who will find the way to exploit young children while in their care and under their control, as I was for eight years in Artane. These men got their satisfaction by a combination of physical force and sadistic brutality.

Looking back, I recall other Brothers such as the Sis, Rowdy, Brother Davaro. They made use of the attractive boys for their pleasure in a way that could seem kind and gentle.

They all came to Artane in the summertime. Some of them, like Sis, Rowdy and Brother Davaro stayed longer, too long.

It was 1953, the year I was, most unfortunately, in the class of the Brother we called Joey Boy. I remember one awful day when I was reported by a monitor to him for swearing. I will always remember his beady look as a perverted smile spread over his handsome face. As he came towards me, his voice wavered. 'Stand up, you pup.' The classroom of almost fifty boys aged eleven fell silent. 'Get out into the back hall, boy. I will make you swear, you'll be sorry you were born. Step out.' In fact I almost ran out. I heard his wavering voice: 'Take off your boots, socks and trousers and lie over the bench, hands flat on the floor. I will teach you a lesson you won't forget.'

He was right; I never have forgotten what he did. First, this sexually depraved Christian Brother used all of his strength to do what he promised he would by flogging my naked buttocks and thighs with a hard leather strap. Before cutting my naked ass, he beat the soles of my bare feet. It was then he pulled my arse between his legs and while he did try to force entry, my cries for help possibly prevented the rape.

But still, I felt him bouncing off my naked buttocks for quite a long, grunting moment. When he had finished I felt a wet and sticky substance on my buttocks and thighs. Thinking it was blood, I felt my arse but when I looked at my sticky wet hand it was not as I had expected it to be, red with blood. It was his semen. Many months later he repeated his sexual abuse in the same way on me in a room just off the practice music room in the long hall. I can still recall his radiant expression that evening as the band played 'The Minstrel Boy', a military march engraved in my memory.

Brother Simon Davaro was in another league. He came to Artane on different occasions as a holiday replacement. When he first came, he was nicknamed the Sting. In later years, his nickname was Angel Face. In my previous writing I have referred to them as two people; the Sting contained his sadistic side, Angel Face the opposite. The affects of abuse are manifold. As I update this memoir, seventeen years after my first book was published, and nine years after Ireland's prime minister formally apologised for what the Christian Brothers and others have done, I now feel able to explore what this man did to me more fully. Brother Simon Davaro reappeared in my life time and again, and it has taken me a long time to come to terms with the impact of what he did, and the way that he did it. He abused me, yes, but he could show a lot of kindness, and a sorrow for what he did.

I was at least nine years old when I first got to know him. It was a beautiful golden autumn evening in late October 1951.

I was in Quickfart's gang along with Jamjar, the Burner,

Blossom and Bloom and many more. The Burner came to me and said, 'You got any conkers, Collie?'

I stood facing him. 'Chestnuts,' I said, real loud, as Jamjar approached us, followed by Blossom and Bloom. They were identical twins, good-looking fair-haired young lads. 'Let's go and fill our bleedin' pockets with conkers, lads.'

'Last over the wall is a rotten swine,' shouted Jamjar.

'Last again, Collie?' said a smiling Quickfart.

'The Sting is on duty with Hellfire, lads. We better hurry,' warned Blossom. I felt scared.

'Who's the bleedin' Sting?' said Jamjar.

'He's a new Brother. He won't go near us.'

'Not half,' muttered Bloom.

I turned to face him. 'How do you know?' I said, eager to find out.

'He had me the other night in the boot room in the dormo. He mauled my bare arse. I couldn't shit or sit down on it, the swine beat me so hard.'

'Why did he do that to you?' I said.

'He caught me ou-ra bed swapping a comic.'

'Come on, lads, fill up, there's loads of bleedin' conkers here. Grab all youse can and let's get back before we're caught.'

'Last one back gives up all his conkers,' shouted Jamjar.

'You got to be joking,' I said. Once again I was last back over the wall on to the parade ground. As I landed I stood, petrified, facing Brother Davaro with a monitor beside him. I was shocked to see all the lads in my gang standing with their hands raised high above their heads facing the wall. 'He's in dormitory five, classroom two, sir. Division sixteen, sir,' said the monitor.

'Your name, boy,' said Brother Davaro, staring at me.

'Patrick Touher, sir. I'm called Collie sir.'

'Report to me, Patrick, after prayers in the dormitory tonight, boy. And don't forget.'

As we marched like boy soldiers from prayers in the beautiful chapel, the beautiful sound of the choir singing in Latin hung in the warm autumn air. Tears welled in my eyes in fear and dread of what would happen to me when I reported to the Brother Davaro at eight that night.

I marched that night to the refectory so fearful of what lay ahead I couldn't eat my supper of bread – which we called yang – hot dripping and tea. I couldn't wait to ask Jamjar how he got on. But I got no chance. The Burner shouted, 'Hey Collie, you are bleedin' in for it, I swear, he's a shaggin' feeler. He almost pulled my prick off. When I swore at him to leave me conkers alone, he beat my naked arse until I broke free of him. He's a bleedin' evil weirdo, Collie, a perverted cunt.'

'A pervert,' I muttered, confused.

'You don't bleedin' understand, do yeh Collie?' said the Burner.

I shook my head.

'But you will tonight. This new geezer, the Sting, he's one shaggin' mauler, Collie,' said Blossom. 'He knelt down over me, pulled my shorts down, my socks came off, so I felt naked though I had me shirt on. I felt his finger up my arsehole.'

'Are you sure it was a finger?' shouted the Burner.

'I'm sure,' said Blossom. 'I rolled out from under him. He just grabbed me. He pushed me over the bed and beat me something awful and flogged my bare feet when he got up off me. I felt my bottom. It was sticky and wet. I'm reporting him.'

'Who would believe you?' said Bloom, looking anxious as he sipped his tea.

'No bleedin' chance, Blossom me pal. There's a lot more than this new geezer, the Sting, getting their pleasure out of us kids. I hear this new bloke is only passing through,' said Burner.

'Yeah, and the shaggin' sooner he passes through the bleedin' better,' said Jamjar. He stared at me a sorrowful look as he gulped from his tin mug. 'You're next, Collie.'

That night as I stood for grace after the meal the sound of almost 900 boys praying aloud moved me to tears. Not of joy but tears of fear of what I'd suffer between prayers and sleep.

I will always remember the thundering sounds of marching feet as 900 boys in hobnail leather boots stamped their feet on the red-tiled floor, keeping in time, waiting for their turn to march out of the refectory to shouts of 'left, left, left right left'. The sound of marching feet is engraved in my memory.

After night prayers in the dormitory and the singing of 'O Sweet Sacrament Divine', I reported as ordered by Brother Davaro. I felt so lonesome.

As was usual several boys stood facing the wall, their hands held high above their heads, waiting to be punished, just as I was. Every night the sounds in the dormitory were of boys crying after suffering severe pain from the beatings on the hands or across the bare buttocks. The sound of crying that began after prayers, and continued after lights out at 10pm, often helped drown out the sound of the wind rattling the tall pull-up windows.

That night I was last to be dealt with. I entered the small claustrophobic bedroom in the corner of the huge dormitory. 'Now close the door, boy, and take off the night-shirt, and come to me, boy.' The Brother was sitting on a chair by a dressing table. He wore a long black cassock with a wide waistband, his collar was white, his dark hair was oily, short, trimmed neatly back and sides. His voice was strangely subdued, I thought. I prayed he would not beat me as I was naked.

I was crying as he pulled me over his lap. His warm hands

were molesting me. He held and squeezed my penis and testicles. I cried out, 'It hurts me, sir.' I could feel him forcing his fingers inside my anus, pushing inside me. I tumbled from his lap on to the floor, then he pulled me between his legs and beat my naked buttocks first with his hand. Then suddenly his weighted leathers crashed excruciatingly off my buttocks. He sounded excited as he kept talking. 'You filthy pup, you mix with brats, you break the rules. I will break you, boy, you pup.' He kept repeating this over and over and over. I'm certain I could see his long, hard penis. It was then I pulled away as he tried to pull me into him. I lay on the floor, my back resting against the bed. He was wiping himself off with his handkerchief. I was totally unaware of the pleasure and relief he had just experienced as I sat there crying.

He was a changed man when he'd calmed down. His voice was soft. He sounded real nice. I almost liked him. 'Stand up, son. I'm so sorry if I hurt you, come to me.' I moved closer. Slowly he embraced me. I couldn't stop crying. My bottom felt wet and sticky, and I was uncertain what it was – whether it was blood or what came from him as he satisfied his hunger and his wild desire for pleasure. He became a different man as he calmly embraced me, hugging me and apologising to me. 'I will never hurt you again, I promise you,' he said.

I couldn't believe how nice he became. His voice became very soft. He actually gave me the feeling he was very sorry as he continued to caress me, hugging my body close to him while all the while I cried in pain.

'Promise me you won't tell anyone about this.' He looked at me waiting for my response.

'I promise, sir,' I cried out in his arms.

'I will never touch you again, I promise you, boy. Now, wipe your eyes. Tell me, are your parents alive?'

I shook my head. 'No, sir, I'm alone, sir. I got no mum or dad, sir!'

'Ahh, so you are a wee orphan. Put your night-shirt on and go back to your bed and remember: tell no one about this, son.'

'Yes, sir.' I couldn't get over how nice he was.

He next came to the school in July 1953. At first, I didn't realise he was the same man as the cruel Sting and neither did he seem to recognise me, one boy out of nearly 900. His voice was soft, smooth and warm. 'Hello. I'm rather new here, son. I'm looking for the Brother General who is in charge over the boys' refectory. Can you help me at all?' His smile was natural, sincere. It enhanced his very handsome good looks. He was tall, slim and must have been in his mid-thirties.

'If you follow me, sir, I will take you to the Reverend Brother General's office, as I work for him.'

As we entered the long refectory, he paused to gaze up at

the huge, long paintings of The Last Supper, the Angelus and many more of the lakes of Killarney and of the Mourne Mountains. I could tell he was amazed and taken by it all.

He stood facing me in the great hall. 'So tell me, what do you do here, and what is your name, son?'

I was really taken in by his soft, smooth voice and his style too. I hoped he had come to stay here. I thought what a change he'd be compared to the Macker, the Bucko, Hellfire, the Apeman, Joey Boy and the most feared of all, the evil Sheriff.

I gave him my name and said, 'But I'm known to everyone, sir, as Collie, cos I like cauliflower, sir. Because we've all got nicknames, even the Brothers, sir.'

'I see, I see. It won't be long before they give me one.' He smiled at me.

'No, sir. Before breakfast tomorrow, sir.'

He laughed aloud and stroked his chin, then swiftly ran his fingers through his silky dark hair. 'So tell me, Collie, what do you do here? Tell me as you take me to the office.'

I noticed my friends Oxo and Minnie making faces at me. I stopped at the steps to the office and explained to him my duties. 'I'm a kitcheners, boy, sir. I help prepare the tables and food, sir. Right now, sir, I've to help make fifty gallons of sweetened tea for the boys' supper, sir.'

'Goodness, that much tea. How do you make it?'

I pointed to the huge copper boilers near Oxo. 'We boil

the water, sir, in them boilers. Then the Drisco, sir, he's Brother General in charge, sir, he brings a sack filled with loose tea. It's not a big sack, sir. The Drisco lowers the sack of tea into the boiling water while we stir it with long wooden paddles like oars, sir. Then the Drisco pours basins of full-cream milk in on top as we stir it, sir. Finally, a basin or a bucket of sugar is added to sweeten it, sir.'

The new Brother gave me a look of amazement and laughed. As he flicked his hair back, he smiled at me. I guess he likes me, I thought. I really liked him. 'What if some of the boys don't take sugar, what do they get?'

'They get the same as we all get, sir. Boiled sweet tea, sir. We call it slash, sir. The bread is called yang, sir.'

He smiled warmly at me, brushed the top of my head with a swift flick of his hand. 'I'll see you around and about. What class are you in?'

'I'm in fourth, sir. Joey Boy is the Brother in charge of it, sir.'

'So tell me, do you like him?'

'No, sir. He's far too cruel on us, sir. I hate him, in fact.'

'Goodness, what a shame. All children should like school. Well, I must go. You better go and stir the tea.'

Oxo was quick off the mark. 'You'd better watch 'im Collie. He likes you.'

Minnie burst out laughing as he stood by the second boiler, stirring the milk into the tea.

'What's so funny? I happen to like the new Brother. He's so nice and friendly and he's real interested in me.'

That drew howls of laughter from Oxo and Minnie. But it didn't stop me from wondering what it would be like to have such a kind and well-spoken man for a father.

Later, a few days later, I guess, Minnie tried to warn me about the new Brother while we were setting the tables for breakfast the next morning. 'There's Angel Face, Collie.'

I looked around but he was gone.

'You got to be careful of him. Oxo warned me about men like him. Just be careful, as he may want to be more than a friend, if you know what I mean.'

'No, I don't, and I really like him. He's different. He's so nice. I am fond of him.'

Minnie faced me. 'Look Collie, we all like him. He *is* different but he won't be kept on here after the summer holidays.'

'Oh, I see, that's it. Why won't he be kept on? Too nice is he?'

'Well, he's far too soft for Artane. He's a different breed, that's all. He's far too smooth, too nice, for this awful place. I'm just warning you not to get too close to him, okay? He quite possibly is only here as a holiday replacement.'

'Sure, okay,' I said.

It wasn't long before he showed his true colours again. It

was a sultry night in the late summer. Most of the tall hard men were away on summer vacation so we expected one of the new Brothers to be on duty. In each of the five dormitories there was a small bedroom on the right as you'd enter and an altar. The altar invariably had beautiful vases of freshly cut blooms from the school gardens. Quickfart, Stewie, Peas, Oxo and Minnie were in the beds closest to me. My bed was in row four. The dormo had 200 wrought-iron beds arranged in long, neat white rows. A central passage divided the dormo in two sections, the altar halfway up on the right, the charge room and washroom to the rear, while the boot room was outside.

As we marched into dormitory four that August night, the Apeman stood at the main entrance as we filed inside. I wondered who the other two Brothers on duty were. Stewie nudged me. 'Guess who's on, Collie.'

'Joey Boy,' I said, hoping I was wrong. I heard Oxo being ordered out to face the wall.

'Bleedin' hell, we're not in the bleedin' dormo yet, and lads are facing the shagging wall,' murmured Stewie.

'The bleedin' wall,' I blurted out too loud.

I feared being noted by one of the many monitors in their book. As we knelt down for night prayers by our bedsides I heard a loud whisper. It was Peas. 'It's Angel Face, look.'

As I cast my eyes to the altar, the tall, handsome relief

52

Brother stood facing us, clutching rosary beads and a hymn sheet. Soon his voice echoed sweetly through the huge dormitory.

'I want all of you boys to join with me in the beautiful hymn, "Slane", or as many refer to it, "Be Thou My Vision",' the Brother began. His voice carried above the great wall of sound. I, like others around me, just preferred to listen to the fantastic voice, rather than join in.

As 'Be Thou My Vision' rang out, I was choked with emotion. By the end I was in tears. The hymn became my favourite, and remains so today.

When the Apeman took his place at the altar as night prayers ended, Angel Face moved away. 'Will the following boys face the wall: the Burner, Oxo, Malone, Touher.' Shit, shit. Nothing bleedin' changes in this prison, I thought. I felt defeated. The Apeman's voice rang out as though to warn us of the danger we face by breaking the rules. 'Before the final prayer and hymn, any boy told to face the wall must keep their hands high above their heads. It is wise to obey the rules. Talking, fooling and kneeling on clothing is strictly forbidden. Boys who choose to break the rules will suffer six of the best for the poor souls in Purgatory. Now let us sing all together "O Sweet Sacrament Divine" after me.'

'Fuck the bleedin' Apeman,' moaned Oxo. 'Let's hope Angel Face deals with us, Collie.'

'You got-a-be kidding us,' said the Burner. 'He's fucking weird.'

My hopes were raised at such a thought. I wondered where Brother Davaro had gone to, while screams from boys getting punished by the Apeman up in the washroom sent shivers running through my body. As I stood with the other boys who faced the wall, my arms ached. I decided to lower them when a voice broke the silence. 'Keep your hands up.' I heard his voice. It was him, my hopes were raised. 'Come in, boy.'

I stared at Brother Davaro as Oxo entered his room. The door banged closed. I waited anxiously. Then I heard shouts, 'Leave me alone, you bleedin' swine. Leave me alone.' The sound of leather crashing off naked flesh always scared me.

The door swung open. Oxo came out, his hands covering his arse. 'I'm bleedin', Collie. He's a bleedin' queer. I warned yeh.'

Just then the Apeman arrived, as though he was anxious to prevent a row. He pointed to Oxo and Peas. 'The two of you report to me every night for a week and walk the centre passage until lights out. You filthy pups.'

'Next.' I looked at the door. Brother Davaro was waiting. I suddenly felt frightened of this new Brother whose smooth voice and soft smile had me wishing he was me dad. Now, as I entered the room, I felt scared. Brother Davaro's voice was soft, though he was flushed. 'I'm sorry for your pal. Oxo, is it?'

'Yes, sir.'

'Well, he swore at me and he's got a very bad record, I hear. You look frightened, Collie. Come sit here beside me.'

I noticed the long, hard leather strap on the chest of drawers. I suddenly feared the pain of it crashing off my naked buttocks. Is he just like the others? I wondered. He eased my cotton night-shirt over my head and, as it fell to the floor, he embraced me. I was shocked by this. After a long, silent moment I felt his lips on me, his hands comforting me. I was in his firm embrace as his lips trailed all over my nakedness while I stood still, fearful of getting flogged. I had no idea what he might do to me, yet I was tearful and too frightened to pull away from him. He pulled me low down on to him. I could feel he was really hard. I was shocked as he placed my hand on it. I pulled my hand away.

I hated men getting close to me, hugging, kissing and fondling me. These acts made my skin crawl. And yet I had a strange tendency to being cradled and molested, even as an eight-year-old in dormo five. The Macker and Hellfire sexually molested me on several occasions as an eight- to ten-year-old. However, I liked Brother Davaro because he was, I believed, different. Each time he came to me, he was very smooth and kind.

Late August the following year I was in dormitory three, I remember the occasion very well. I was returning from the toilets, which were, in fact, outside the dormitory off the landing. As I re-entered the dormo, I heard a loud whisper calling me. 'Collie.' Angel Face summoned me to his room. It was a small, well-furnished room. His voice was soft. His smile lit up his handsome features. 'Are you lonely? You look frightened, son. Are you? Do not be afraid of me, son. Are you afraid, boy?'

I lied, of course. I guess it didn't always pay to tell the truth, I thought.

'Come and lie down beside me.' I got this strange but very nice scent from him. As he drew me close into him, I barely felt him lift my night-shirt. On this occasion he drew me on to his naked chest. I felt really odd. I had never been this close to someone before, never held in such a tender warm embrace. But I wondered what would happen now. I was fearful, yet I felt secure, insofar that I trusted that he would in no way make me suffer excruciating pain. That thought comforted me to a degree. But when he lay down on top of me I could feel him. It was then I feared him.

I began to cry out. 'Please, sir, please not down there, sir, it hurts. Please.'

I feared he was about to forcefully penetrate me. But I could not prevent him as he was on top of me, unlike the time with Joey Boy in the long hall. That time I struggled free from the perverted evil he was, but not without suffering a severe beating. But this is different, I thought. I can't fight him or hope to crawl out from under his body. So I cried out as he drew me up to him. He began beating himself off with loud groans.

When he let me go, I had no pain. He did not hurt me, physically at least. Emotionally, he did. Enough for me to never forget him. He got satisfaction from holding me naked as he enjoyed self-masturbation against me.

After a long silent moment, Brother Davaro brushed back his silky hair. His smile widened. 'I hope I haven't hurt you.'

'No, sir, I'm fine, sir.' I lied, as I was really scared.

'You better get to bed, son.'

I remember the final moment that warm night as he stood there brushing his fine crop of hair, facing the mirror on the dressing table. I was naked. My night-shirt was between his feet. I remained seated on the edge of his bed, thinking how smooth and gentle he was. How vastly different he was to the other Brothers, yet still I was scared. I was crying when he moved away. I reached down to retrieve my night-shirt. I felt his warm hands holding me. His scent was warm fragrance, his voice soft and very comforting, like his smile.

'Are your parents living?'

'No, sir.' I was anxious to get dressed. I was relieved to get my night-shirt on. It helped me feel better as I really felt odd standing naked in front of him.

'So you are an orphan?'

I nodded yes.

'I want to be your friend. Do you like chocolate?'

'Yes, sir.'

'And sweets?'

I nodded yes.

He embraced me, hugging me warmly, close to him. 'You better go to bed. I will look after you before I leave here. Sleep well, now. I'll remember you.'

'Yes, sir. I'll remember you too, sir.'

'Promise me.'

I looked up at him. His smile was soft. 'I promise, sir.'

It was a promise I faithfully kept in my dreams and nightmares.

For me, not getting a severe beating that night from Brother Davaro was a great relief. But the fact he was leaving us made no difference to my life or that of my pals, as the truth is there was always the very evil hard-core band of Brothers who enforced the strict, rigid military system. Fear was the key.

5

The day I left Artane memories flooded back to me as I stood at the bus stop opposite the main gates and stared at the great school building that so dominated the area. I looked up at the clear blue sky, and watched a flock of birds flying over. As the number 42 bus pulled up, I smiled as I hopped on the back. 'Free as a bird!' I said to myself with a soft smile.

I sat downstairs on the bus, clutching my brown paper parcel. Suddenly I heard the conductor shout, 'Fare, son! Where are you going, lad?'

My mind was all at sea.

The conductor asked again, 'Where are you going, lad?'

'Where are you going to?' I replied.

The conductor looked amazed and spoke sharply. 'The Pillar, mate. It says it on the front, lad. The Pillar in the city centre.'

At least I knew where I was going to get off. I paid my two pence and sat tight.

When I stood up to get off I noticed the conductor staring me up and down. I knew then that I stood out in my Artane clothes. I tried to read the address Segoogee gave me, and I cursed his rotten handwriting. It was even worse than mine. I glanced about. I noticed a guard gazing at the new spring wear in the window of Clery's store. Filled with apprehension, I spoke quietly to him. 'Please, sir, could you help me find this place? I'm lost, sir.'

He looked down at me. He was tall – a double for the Macker, I thought. He smiled at me and led me across the road. We stopped in front of the Palm Grove ice-cream parlour. He didn't ask me if I would like an ice-cream cone: he simply went in and got me one. I was lost for words, but to me his kindness was the mark of a great man.

He didn't asked me where I came from. As I followed him to the corner where the Irish Press office stood in Middle Abbey Street, he stopped and said, 'You're from Artane School, son?' He smiled, and I nodded to him in response. Then he pointed to the place where I was to stay. 'You're home, son. I'm sure they'll take care of you.' Then he nodded and disappeared into the crowd. For a long moment I stood staring emptily after him.

I looked up at the tall red-brick building. The sign over it read The Catholic Boys' Home. It did not impress me. I was frightened. I felt out of my depth. I just wanted to go home to Artane.

I found it difficult to hold back the tears as I walked up the few steps. There was a long room in front of me, and I could smell tea being prepared. There were two long dining tables with white cloths – a miniature Artane refectory, I thought. I heard voices. A door opened on my right. 'Come this way, boy.' I stood in the office, nervously gazing at the cream-painted walls.

An elderly man came to meet me. 'So you're the new boy from Artane.' I half smiled and said, 'Yes, sir. I got lost.' He looked me in the eye and spoke with a warmth I had rarely known. 'Many have done the very same thing, my boy. A darn pity a Brother doesn't come with you. Perhaps they're too busy, son.'

The Catholic Boys' Home was mainly for boys aged sixteen and over. It was a kind of stopping-off place in the city for boys who had left school and had no home to go to. We paid seven shillings and sixpence a week for our keep. The food was very basic and no better than what we were used to in Artane. But we did have hot showers.

I remember that first evening at tea quite clearly. I sat down with lads whom I spent years with in Artane – some of whom I didn't like. But there were others who I didn't know. The first nickname I heard being shouted was 'Brown Tango' – a chap from Africa in his late teens or a bit older. He lorded it a bit, and perhaps he thought he was better than us from

Artane. I didn't like the look he gave me, and I believe he bumped against me on purpose, to knock my mug of tea out of my hand. He certainly threw himself about. Oddly enough, the ex-Artaners did not behave like that.

It was typical Artane food: bread and margarine and a mug of sweet tea in the evening; breakfast was different though – we had porridge.

After tea I was shown to my dormitory on the third floor. The front of the dormo looked out on to Middle Abbey Street; the back looked down into the North Lotts, where we watched couples courting and fondling each other at night among the winos. From my bed I could see the clock over the Irish Independent office; and I was happy about that, because I had never had a watch!

It was noisy in the dormitory, and something I'd never be able to get used to, I told myself through my tears. I cried as much now as ever I did for my lost childhood, tears of loneliness and self-pity. There was no real sense of being free. In the dormitory were two long rows of beds made of tubular steel and painted grey. The walls were painted yellow and dark green. As I put away my few belongings I was dreading the future. I just wanted to go out and get the bus back to Artane.

The lads acted in a boisterous way, and at times many were very rowdy. Later I was shocked to see lads from Artane running up and down naked, some of them fondling or messing about with their private parts and generally showing off to others how big their penis was! This was a really new experience for me.

I got off the bed as a lad came towards me. It was Fatser. 'Want me to show yeh the city? Come on.' I looked at him. I remembered the day he broke my nose over a silly matter in 1955. I had gone to the Sheriff who was in charge on parade that day. He had snapped at me sharply. 'What do you want me to do, boy?' His next remark stayed with me for ever. 'Stand up for yourself, boy. Be brave and hit back or kick back twice as hard. Fight him, boy!'

As the days passed I began to find my way around the city. We were brought to services in the Pro-Cathedral: sodality, the Rosary, and Benediction. Hearing again the choir singing the Latin hymns moved me emotionally, making me more homesick for Artane. As I stood up after the Benediction was over, the man in charge of us in the boys' home said, 'Confessions are being heard now.' I better go, I thought.

When I entered the confessional my mind raced over the past few weeks. Gosh, I've nothing to confess, I said to myself. It's a waste of time.

I heard the little hatch go across. I smiled, as I had no bad thoughts and had committed no dirty deeds. The middle-aged priest spoke clearly: 'How long since your last confession?'

'Not long, Father: a few weeks.'

The priest continued, 'Well, lad, what have you got for me? Anything to confess?'

'No, Father.' And I thought that was that.

As though he didn't believe me, he raised his deep voice. 'Do you attend all services: Mass, Holy Communion, novenas, and your sodality?'

'Yes, Father, at all times, Father.' I thought that was it, but more was to come.

The priest grunted. 'Ah sure, 'tis too good, lad, you are. Tell me, do you use swear-words?'

'No, Father, the Brothers taught us not to, sir.'

'Do you play with yourself at all?'

'No, Father. I play with others, though.'

'Tell me, do you see the others play with themselves at all?'

I was baffled. 'You mean in the snooker room or in the park?'

He raised his voice, angrily I thought. 'No, damn it, anywhere, boy! Did you see them play with their bodies?'

Suddenly the thought struck me. 'Yes, Father, quite often.'

'Where did all this take place, my son?'

'Oh, mostly up in the dormitory, and at times in the shower room, Father. I don't understand it, though.'

'I see, I see … I'll have to visit there. 'Tis better that you don't understand, lad, as it will only corrupt your mind. And remember to continue to go to Holy Mass and all the services. 'Tis a mortal sin to perform dirty acts with another, to indulge in self-abuse of your own body for enjoyment or fulfilment. Remember to keep your hands joined when temptation strikes. It's Satan's way of corrupting the mind. Now for your sins, say five decades of the Rosary and do the Stations of the Cross at least once a week.'

As I settled down in my new home I found it difficult to shake off the shackles of Artane. I was glad about some aspects of the boys' home. I had my own toothbrush, soap and towel – a big change from sharing with so many others. I kept going to church services; I was an emotional and institutionalised ex-Artaner, out of my depth in a big city – though I was finding my feet.

I began to fall in love with the city. I walked along Bachelor's Walk on summer evenings, dreaming of what I wanted to be. I was driven by a desire to be someone great – to achieve greatness. This meant that I started to take a closer look at myself, especially when I was out in the city alone. I took note of how other teenagers dressed, and it wasn't long before I realised that I could never really look much different in my Artane Sunday outfit, a heavy serge suit. I longed to have the money but I wondered how I could get enough of it.

One thing that I was certain about was that I was different in some way from the other ex-Artaners with whom I shared the facilities in the Catholic Boys' Home. I was a bit of a loner, and rather choosy about who I mixed with. I was old-fashioned in my ways and I was very particular about my cleanliness and how I appeared to others.

But even as I adjusted to life outside Artane, I was still plagued by nightmares and sleepwalking, which I continued to be for many years afterwards, as I found it so difficult to shake off the draconian system that I had endured. The best advice I received was from a priest who came to visit us in the boys' home. Father Brien explained to me that the only way you can truly hope to recover from your experience in Artane is to change your ways. I remember the evening so well as I sat facing the soft-spoken, affable, middle-aged man talking to me about how I could travel abroad. I smiled at him. 'You are afraid of change and you believe it's not possible,' he said. I was quick to agree with him, but he wouldn't let go and said, 'You need a way out of your nightmare experience of Artane. You are naive, lonely and you are a very institution-alised young man. You will not break away from that experience unless you are willing to fight it. Travel, young man, see the world, learn new ways, meet new people and make new friends. That's what you need.'

He drew hard on his pipe then exhaled. My eyes followed

the smoke as it rose to the ceiling. Father Brien stood up, clutching his pipe, and smiled at me. He began to move away and then, as though he'd forgot something, he turned back to me and said, 'I sincerely hope you make it, and find a sweet young girl while you're at it. You certainly could do with a good break, lad. God bless you.'

As he went on his way, like the passing cloud of smoke, I wondered just how, or where, I could get the money to travel.

$\mathcal{b}$

On my first day at work I got the early bus out to Fairview, carrying with me the handwritten note Segoogee had given me. I showed it to the conductor, and he let me off at Edge's Corner.

I looked about and saw the sign over a shop: Milk – Dairy – Brennan's. I went in, and suddenly a big, stout woman entered the shop. She spoke rather loudly and abruptly. 'Are you from Artane Industrial School, boy?' As I looked down at my shoes and clothes I supposed they told it all. She reached out her fat hand. Her grip was firm and she left butter on my fingers. 'I'm Mrs Brennan. They're expecting you in the bakery. You'll like Mr Bradley. He's a countryman from Derry.' She looked at me. 'I suppose you're from Dublin?'

'No, ma'am, I'm from Artane School.'

She smiled and said, 'Bill will take you to the bakery, son.'

She reminded me of Bridget Doyle in Barnacullia.

For a few moments I stood gazing at the place in which I

was to begin my working life. What a bleak-looking house, I thought as I entered the yard. However, there was a well-kept lawn, and the garden had a spring freshness about it, with tall palm trees on my left, then the bakery. As I approached I became apprehensive as I heard male voices shouting very crude and vulgar words, some I had never heard before. My mind was filled with all sorts of fears.

I heard a man's voice with a northern accent. 'Hello, son. Are you the new boy from Artane?'

On top of the old stone steps that led into the house stood a very tall middle-aged man, who was to be my first employer. 'Come on in, son, and tell us about yourself and Brother Shannon.'

Mr Bradley seemed huge as I stood looking up at him in the front room: taller than the Sheriff and even the Macker, I reckoned. 'Are you ready, Pauline? I want you to meet our new baker from Artane.' I shook hands with his wife, who was young and very attractive. I was taken by surprise when she gave me a hug and a friendly kiss on the cheek. Her smile and warmth made me long for a mother's love. 'Now, you'll have some breakfast with us before my husband brings you down to meet the lads. They're both ex-Artane boys, and they're both from Dublin, like myself.' I sat down to the first bacon, sausage and egg breakfast I had ever seen.

Soon I met the other boys I was to work with. Eddie was

a fair-haired young man in his twenties, a Dublin lad from Whitehall. I got on with Eddie much more than with Matt, his deputy, who came from the inner city. They treated me like an errand boy. When Matt ran out of cigarettes he would order me to go out and look for as many butts as I could find around Fairview, and often I would stop a person and beg a cigarette from them. Knowing Matt, I was afraid to come back without any.

The work itself wasn't hard, though I found it monotonous, and the baking powder gave me a runny nose and head colds. The hours were short, but getting up so early made each day seem long. Sometimes the bakers would start work at three in the morning, and I'd have to be in at half four. Getting up so early made me cranky, but within a few months I was settling down to the way of things. I can clearly recall those early days, stirring the buttermilk left in big tall milk churns by Merville Dairies. After the bake I often sat on a bag of soft Boland's flour and ate a chunk of white griddle bread and homemade apple pie.

I found it difficult to fit in at work. I couldn't relate at all to people who were not ex-Artaners, and I had no idea about girls. I often irritated the men. Eddie complained that I talked too much and sang too many of the songs I learnt in school. I had formed a habit of whistling or singing 'The

Croppy Boy' and 'The Boys of Wexford'. One day I couldn't stop laughing at Mick Bradley as he was making griddle bread with Eddie, and he spoke seriously to me about my ways. 'One day, Pat, you're going to find a great deal of trouble, the way you go on here, singing and laughing when spoken to. You give the impression that you either have a wee chip on your shoulder or that you're odd.'

As I went home that evening I felt ashamed at what Mr Bradley had said. I wasn't whistling as I walked either. I began to realise that I was not wanted.

The thoughts of being rejected frightened me. If an ex-Artane lad was rejected by his work because he did not fit in he was returned to Artane if he had no family to look after him. Being an orphan, I would have had to return, as I would not be able to pay for my keep. That night as I lay down to sleep I felt unwanted, but I prayed as I had learnt to pray in Artane. I made up my mind that I would not be going back. I knew I could fight to achieve that end, and, thank God, I did. I was bitterly determined to succeed.

By the end of 1958, I was more settled in work. Mrs Bradley was very kind. She must have felt sorry for me. She brought me into the house some evenings to feed me. How I loved that!

I walked to work from the boys' home to the little bakery in Fairview, getting up at about four, with no breakfast, just a few 'prairie sandwiches' to take with me. The lads often had no lunch with them, and Eddie and Matt would be glad to share mine. Eddie would often remark, 'For Jesus's sake, Pat, could they not find a bloomin' thing to put in them?'

'Bread and margarine? What yeh expect for seven shillings and sixpence a week?' said Matt. 'Ham and bleedin' eggs, no way!'

I liked Eddie, though often he'd get ratty with me. A favourite expression of his was 'Look, Paddy, for feck's sake, d'yeh want me to lose me rag? Do yeh?'

Matt was quite something else. He showed all the signs of an Artaner. He enjoyed ordering people about, and he loved his authority; he spoke down to everyone when there were people about. He was more at home and normal when he found himself in trouble, as the times when Eddie didn't come in to work. Matt would need me to help him through the day, and he was a better bloke then.

One day I was working with the boss and Eddie. During tea break neither Mick nor Eddie had anything to eat with them. We never stopped for long, as there was always bread or whatever it was to come out of the oven. I was the only one who brought lunch with me. The boss looked at me. I was apprehensive about offering him some of my prairie sandwiches. Mick glanced at me. Putting down the cup he said, 'Goddamn it, Pat, can I have one?' Eddie laughed. I watched as Mick opened the bread up. 'Is this all they feed you with? Damn shame.' He looked me in the eye and spoke softly. 'You know, son, you'll have to find a real home. You're living far too long with Artane.'

'He reeks of Artane!' Eddie shouted.

'You need a good woman to sort you out, Pat,' Mick said, as he turned to face Eddie. 'What do you think?'

Eddie almost choked on his Woodbine, and then responded, 'If there was a room in my place me ma would look after him.'

Mick reacted instantly. 'Ah, sure, 'tis the old story, Eddie. If I had the money I'd buy you a jar. If only I had this and that, I'd do wonders, Eddie.'

Some days later I was asked to do the garden and paint the bakery windows, as there was not enough work in the bakery for the three of us. I was asked to come up for tea by Pauline. I began to get the feeling for real home life as I made myself comfortable. Mick Bradley asked me if I'd like to see around. How could I say no? As I stood in their large bedroom I imagined what it would be like to sleep in a nicely painted room all to myself, with carpet on the floor. As I meandered back from the Bradleys' house I felt happy within myself but realised that that kind of happiness is too instant, and once I got back to the boys' home I was back down to earth.

*

In September 1958 Dublin got to the All-Ireland final in Croke Park. My boss, Mick Bradley, was on a high. The bakery was decked out in the red-and-white colours of Derry and the blue of Dublin. I didn't see Mick for a few weeks after Dublin's great victory. When I did see him he was on crutches. He had broken his leg trying to climb a wall outside Croke Park to get in to the game.

In those days I was an ardent Dublin supporter. I recall seeing the Macker, the Sheriff and a few more Brothers at the games. On many an occasion ex-Artaners, especially those living in Sheriff Street and the Catholic Boys' Home, threw apples or bottles at the Brothers. The Sheriff got hit on many occasions, yet it never changed him one bit. I realise my feeling might be incomprehensible to some, perhaps a complex result of the abuse, but it hurt me to see the Brothers being attacked like that. It was never my attitude.

It was during the August holiday Monday in 1958 that I paid a nostalgic visit to the Doyles up in Barnacullia. I set off early from the home with my old pal Seamus, having borrowed Fatser's bike, as Seamus had decided he would like to make a day of it and leave after breakfast.

We decided to stop at the old schoolhouse in Sandyford and take a walk around the playground before turning up the old road to Barnacullia and Glencullen. We put away our bicycles; locks and chains were not necessary then. We walked the road, up to the old grocer himself, the Tiller Doyle. Bald on top, a touch of silver along the sides, he shouted out: 'I remember ye, boys. Oh, God be good to those who return to thank those who cared for them!'

I said goodbye to him in a whisper, but never did the words mean so much. All my childhood dreams and fond memories came flooding to my mind. I could only nod to Seamus as we walked on up the climb until we reached the turning of the road that led up to the row of cottages on the hill. The track, as we called it when we lived there, was still the same. I stopped at the well where as a young boy I fetched buckets of water for Bridget Doyle. I could see that Seamus was gazing down the hill and across to Carty's Green. I knew that he was reliving his lost childhood, as I was.

Mrs Doyle looked as healthy as ever as I put my arms around her. I wondered where Margaret and her brother John were. Before I could ask, in walked Margaret, followed by John – tall, thin but strong-looking, and smiling. As I greeted them, Margaret first, my heart missed a beat. As I turned to shake John's hand I couldn't believe how much older than me he looked. I just smiled and cried with joy. I thought of Margaret as my sister, and how I wished to God that she truly was.

Mr Doyle was seated by the open fire in an old well-worn

armchair, smoking his pipe; Shep the dog, his muzzle now grizzled with grey, was by his feet.

Bridget was putting homemade apple pie and bread into the oven. She turned to her daughter Margaret. 'Why don't you take the lads across the hillside for an hour. Tea will be ready when you return. 'Twill do yeese good, sure. Be back by five o'clock.'

Just then the old clock on the black dresser struck four. The sweet sounds of the chimes brought back fond memories when I was one of the family and believed I was one of them and not just some kid passing through. 'Ye better be going before it's time to come back, Margaret,' Bridget said as she closed the oven door. She raised herself upright, wiping her hands in her colourful pinafore. The beautiful aroma of the apple pie and homemade buttermilk bread in the oven filled my lungs, made me feel hungry. I wished – not for the first time – as we made our way from the cosy hillside cottage that Bridget was my mother.

After the walk with Margaret, we had tea and then I said goodbye to the Doyles. I stood on the green hilltop for a better view of the picturesque landscape that opened up before my eyes. All the beauty of Barnacullia to Glencullen, and behind us lay the ever-changing colours of green and gold that formed part of the Dublin hills, and, below

Sandyford, Stepaside to Enniskerry. My dreams were real. The visions I harboured as a prisoner in Artane Industrial School were not imaginary after all. I smiled sadly as I thought that so much I had missed of a normal life as a child can't ever be brought back.

What I would have given for a foothold in this beautiful hillside, a cosy cottage home with an open log fire, a dog like Shep, a clock on the dresser and a mother like Bridget with a heart of gold. To come home to the aroma of fine cooking where I could sit and dwell and dream by the fireside sure would be real nice, I thought.

I stared down the hillside. Although I was free, each night I had awful nightmares, I walked in my sleep. I shouted and screamed until perspiration dripped from me. Then there would come the calming voice of the kid holding me. 'You are all right, Paddy, you're back from hell or wherever it was you were at. Come on back to bed.'

For a long, silent moment, alone with myself in paradise, my thoughts ran wild, ran free in my childhood days walking down the hillside with my pals, in the gold of autumn, trundling through the piles of crisp fallen leaves and collecting pocketfuls of shiny chestnuts – gosh, at that moment, though I was free, I wept, as I muttered I wish to God that Artane was really only a very bad dream.

As I meandered across the hillside to meet Seamus I cried,

yet I wanted to scream and shout out this is where I lost out, my childhood snatched, stolen and brutally crushed by state, power and fear. 'Fear of the collar,' I muttered as Seamus approached me.

'Talking to yourself as usual,' said Seamus grinning at me.

'What do you mean?' I asked him. 'Well, nothing much really, except you've always talked in your sleep. Come on, Paddy,' he said, 'let's go home. A shame, I could have stayed forever up here. It's so peaceful, so clean.'

I nodded in full agreement, wishing the same things from life as him.

On our return home, Seamus never said a word. The few times that I glanced at him I got the gut feeling he was thinking of how different life as a child growing up in Barnacullia would have been and what he had lost out on, as I did.

I realised just then how difficult it would be just getting used to life on the outside. I wondered: would I make it?

7

The Catholic Boys' Home was a four-storey Georgian building, red brick with a very neglected appearance. It was in a terraced row of Georgian buildings with below-level basements. It was the wishes of the Board of Management that we should look for proper lodgings, and we were encouraged not to make the hostel our permanent home. There was no television to enjoy after work. I played hurling and football, though I began to like soccer, which had been forbidden at Artane. I loved playing the matches that were quickly organised by our soccer fanatics, John and Seamus.

As I recall, there was no such thing as unemployment pay or dole at the time. All Artaners were skilled tradesmen and, what's more, we didn't mind hard work or getting up early. This stood us well in tough times though I had so little money.

The Catholic Boys' Home became a meeting place for Artaners who lived in digs or who had joined the army. I knew of many lads at the time who had lost their jobs and found it hard to deal with people or to fit in, who simply got fed up and joined the army. Many went to England to join up. But wherever they chose to go they brought their skills with them.

The dormitory I was placed in had approximately twenty-four beds, all wrought iron painted green. To match the walls I guess, which were a faded cream and dark green. The dining room was painted similarly – deep cream, and below the dado rail a deep awful dark green, more suited to a toilet, which were also painted cream and dark green. Not to spoil things I guess! Evening tea began at 6pm.

As the weeks passed by I was very disheartened by this awful place they called the Catholic Boys' Home. A shelter for young Catholics without proper moorings and rife with sexual abuse.

I walked in my sleep. This caused me many problems as I crept into other lads' beds in my sleep. It was okay when they turned out to be ex-Artaners, but not so good when they were total strangers. I was reported and summoned to the office and threatened with dismissal.

The thoughts of me being left homeless scared me, yet in reality what could I do to prevent myself from sleepwalking? I hated my life and the Catholic Boys' Home.

*

One evening I decided to take a shower, certain I was alone. Once under the shower, I felt the heat of another behind me. His voice was soft, deep but breathless. I realised it was Brown Tango. He said, 'I've been waiting for you. Now the time has come. You are so handsome, I want you. I'm go-na have ye, and we're alone, Collie.'

As he embraced me, I knew I had to fight my way out of this. But how, with what? I was naked. He was taller and stronger than me. 'Please leave me alone. Please,' I cried. He was trying desperately to force himself on me. I struggled, we both fell to the floor. I heard voices. I shouted, 'The Burner, help me. Please, please.'

Brown Tango swore at me. 'Bastard. I will kill you and them if they come near us.'

'Are you okay, Collie?' It was the Burner and Stewie.

I cried out, 'Please help me. Please get 'im away from me. Please help.'

Stewie dived in on top of Brown Tango followed by the Burner. A fierce fight broke out. I stood up. The Burner was lying beneath the shower. He'd slipped and hit his head on the tiled floor as Stewie fought Brown Tango. I decided to help him and pull Brown Tango to the floor. It was one fight I knew I had to win.

Stewie called out, 'Check to see if anyone's about. Quick, I can't hold this geezer down much longer ...'

'Watch it,' I shouted to Stewie. I was too late. Brown Tango got Stewie in a head lock. I shouted for Sean, hoping he'd come in. I was so relieved when he hurried in to help Stewie. Stewie gave Tango a punch smack in the eye. 'That's for tormenting my pal Collie. Go near him ever again and you'll be sorry,' said Stewie. He pushed Brown Tango against the wall. 'Let's beat it ou-ra this queer's face.'

I looked at Stewie. 'Listen, thanks for your help, I'd have been done for only for yeh.' Stewie put an arm around me. I felt safe, though I was naked. He laughed as he said, 'He's after your arse, Collie. He's a violent fucker, and a dangerous one too.'

I began to get dressed. I felt good in Stewie's company. When he spoke again I could sense the seriousness in his voice. 'If that Brown Tango goes near you again and there's no one around, get the hell out and tell the cops. I mean it. I won't always be around, Collie. I'm on shift work and I'm going to England next week.'

My heart missed a beat. 'Are your folks over there?'

He stood facing the cracked mirror, combing his hair. His voice was soft.

'No, no. My parents live here. I don't get along with my pa. He's a docker and he's always full of booze. Do you remember Oxo?'

I felt my spirits raise. 'Sure I do.'

'Well, I'm going to London to stay with him. The bleedin' money is five times more than I get here. Oxo says the English people he works with are far more Christian and human than the shower over here.' Stewie continued. 'Look, Collie. This is not a safe place for the likes of you. Your good looks will draw a certain type to you. Brown Tango is vicious and violent. And you are a good-looking bloke, and I guess you spent quite a bit of time on your knees in Artane. It wasn't all prayer meetings you were kneeling for and I should know. A few of the Brothers tried to force their hard-on up mine; I know they tried it on you. Remember the night we got caught collecting conkers ...'

I said, 'Yeah. Of course.'

'Well, he actually poked his long finger up my arse, and the pervert stroked my privates. My guess, he got what he was after up yours, am I right?'

'No, not really. But he tried. and then he flogged me while I was naked with his leather and hands. Then he embraced me after he calmed down. He became a real nice man. How's that do you think, the sudden change I mean.'

I faced Stewie as he shuffled about. I could see that my question embarrassed him. 'Okay,' he said eventually. 'I'll explain it to you since you don't understand the flippin' reason: certain types of men prefer to have sex with young males. They enjoy molesting and even abusing us kids. They get pleasure over naked boys in the Saturday showers. Remember, do yeh?'

'Of course. How could I ever forget. I walk in my sleep, I suffer awful nightmares.'

'Who are you telling, you got into my bed the other night, Collie. If you were a girl I'd been on top of yeh in a flash. Nothing weird or queer in that, Collie.'

I was amazed at him. 'Why is that, I mean, what is the difference?'

His expression changed. 'Look Collie, you are really very naive, you are different to us.'

'You think I'm queer?' I said.

He burst out laughing. As he came closer, he put an arm around me. 'No, you're not a queer, but you are fucked up. In your head I mean. You need to find a nice girl and learn how to give her pleasure.'

I was confused. 'What do yeh mean by that? Can you explain?'

He gasped, laughed at me and said, 'Oh shit, you want a bleedin' demonstration or what? Look Collie, you're a pal. But me Ma couldn't explain that, never mind me Da, as he's never sober. But if I ever find out, I promise I'll tell you.'

I never felt safe inside the Catholic Boys' Home. Just going to the bathroom was – to my horror – a new experience for me.

There I would see young teenagers masturbating with each other and fondling each other. I never hung about as I felt they were committing mortal sin. In fact, I was scared to get involved in or indulge in any form of sexual playacting for fear of committing sin. I believed in the teachings of the Holy Catholic Church, and I kept going to Sunday Mass and all the services. I prayed to God for help and I relied on my faith in God to help me get through each day.

The small bakery I worked in was about one mile from the city centre. There was no transport at 4.30am so I walked, or I marched as many people commented on the way I walk. As though you are a soldier, they'd say. An early start brought its own problems to me, as I was back in the Catholic Boys' Home early in the day. Each dormitory had a snooker table or two, or table tennis. One afternoon I was practising snooker alone. I was leaning over the table when I heard movement behind me. As I tried to stand up, I felt hands pulling my trousers down. I heard a voice say, 'We got him, Anto.'

'He's mine,' said Anto. 'Let's get him.'

I was uncertain as to what was going to happen next. Then a voice said, 'We're only messing with you, Collie. No need to fight us, it's just a bit of fun.' As I was pushed flat face down, my pants were stripped from me. I could feel my bottom and anus being massaged. 'He's got such a nice tight arse.' I recognised this voice as belonging to an ex-Artaner. Suddenly they got rough.

'His arse is mine and I'm getting a piece of it,' said Anto.

I felt a knife cold on my flesh. I couldn't move at all. They were sitting on my back, my legs were held. 'I'm after you, Anto,' said the ex-Artaner.

I felt the pointed flick knife prodding or being pushed into my skin. My arse was being molested, I'm certain it was by their hands. I heard the door pushed open and voices. A sudden relief swept through my naked body as the voices got closer and clearer. I knew some of them. A voice I knew shouted, 'What are yeh doing to him, Anto? He's my pal, yeh bleedin' queer cunt.'

It was my friend Mick and his gang who started to beat the crap out of these sexually depraved misfits. I stood up just as Mick and Sean attacked Anto and the ex-Artaner. As the fight went on, blood was spilt. I waded into the ex-Artaner and put the boot in, Artane-style. I never liked big Anto. He was a real bully and a gang leader. There were too many like him and Brown Tango in the Boys' Home.

Free from Artane, I found life very difficult. My new home scared me. I had no one to turn to except a few ex-Artaners. I could not put my trust in those men who helped run the Boys' Home, as I felt scared of them, particularly when I found myself alone with one of 'em. I realised much of what Stewie told me was true. Places such as Catholic Boys' Homes were unsafe for young men like me. I found it very difficult to make friends with anyone, except ex-Artaners, as we had a great deal in common I guess. When the men I worked with in the small home bakery told me I reeked of Artane I realised I had to change my ways and the way I dressed. I had so much to learn from the way I addressed people, to the way I spoke, and the awful habit I had of laughing at people whose company I was in. This quite often caused me many problems.

Being free from Artane Industrial Christian Brothers School was in many ways just like being set free from a state prison. Looking back to that time, I believe that to be true. I was set free from a state-run institution where I'd been kept for eight years from the age of eight to the age of sixteen. I had been taken from a normal loving home in the hillside to a very violent and physical, brutal life of prayer, punishment and sexual abuse.

When I slept my dreams were shattered and turned to incredible nightmares. The nightmares, as I recall, seemed so real. The faces in them were of the same hard core of Brothers I feared most of all. The men in black chasing me in my awful dreams-turned-to-nightmares were not simply my demons: they were real men such as the Sheriff, the Bucko, Hellfire, and the Macker. Christian Brothers who so often inflicted excruciating pain and abuse to so many boys in their care.

Life outside of Artane Industrial Christian Brothers School was more difficult to come to terms with than I ever imagined. In reality I was a very naive and gullible young man, totally ignorant of the facts of life, who was sadly very institutionalised. I harboured visions of me joining a sheltered life in a big way. The shadow of Artane I soon realised was to be a long one and would haunt me wherever I travelled.

The main reason I hated the Catholic Boys' Home was quite simply because of bullies such as Brown Tango and a total lack of any privacy. It was nothing more than a Catholic boys' sex club where decent young lads were abused.

I found the first year away from Artane the hardest. I honestly had too much to learn about a normal life, the way to behave, how to act normal. I was always acting as though I was somebody else. Perhaps in reality I was, because I really didn't know who I was or where I came from. I still don't.

8

I was having a fair number of problems in the Catholic Boys' Home towards the end of my first year there. I knew I had to start looking for digs, but I had another problem, one that was to cause me a great deal of bother throughout my life, and that was money, or the lack of it.

I was looking for digs with Fatser. We were up near the Phoenix Park, at a big red-bricked house. I got frightened and told Fatser to go up to the house without me. He shouted, 'Paddy, we're up, come on, will yeh!' The big hall door opened, and a tall woman with a Cork accent said, 'It's two pounds, seven shillings and sixpence per week sharing for full board. Laundry will be two shillings a week extra.' Well, I roared laughing and ran. I was earning only two shillings less than that for working six days, even though it was rarely more than six hours a day. I knew I could never afford to move into fancy lodgings.

Carmella O'Grady, who acted as my adopted godmother

and brought some hope and light while I was in Artane, was an educated and elegant woman, as were her daughters, Joan, Carine and Elizabeth – far and away too educated for Minnie and my other pals. I visited them almost every Saturday since I left Artane and I was allowed to bring pals from the Catholic Boys' Home. After each visit to them I came away feeling I'd learned something.

It was January 1959. Christmas had not been great, but a visit to the O'Gradys in Ballsbridge was a highlight, and, like all visits before, it was a lovely occasion. Whenever Minnie came out with me he generally broke down laughing, so much so that Carmella was amazed one Saturday as she served tea to see Minnie laughing so hard that tea came out his nostrils! I was just as bad. I remember the tall, dark-suited Dr John Francis standing there looking at the pair of us. He was a fine, well-built and elegant man. Carine was concerned now as she spoke to us. 'What's so funny, Patrick? Is it us, or something we said?' How could I tell her that it was? Our inexperience to communicate was the problem!

I explained that Minnie and I tended to laugh at a lot of things that were strange to us, and indeed the whole concept of having tea served to us ex-Artaners on the lawn was simply too much to take. As I look back on the style of things at the O'Grady home in Dublin 4, it does make me smile. In some ways they did help me to be ambitious and to style myself like them. I knew I could never be like them, but at least I found that the more time I spent in their company, the more I would learn from their ways.

In the early spring of 1959 I was lonely and sick with toothache and gum disease, which I had suffered a lot with in Artane. I was sleepwalking often too, as were many other lads. I regularly woke up in some other chap's bed. On one occasion I woke up lying naked on top of this chap who slept at the far end of the dormitory. He was known as Danno, a fine, dark-haired, handsome chap, not an ex-Artaner. He had his arms wrapped around me and he was talking in his sleep. Well, I was scared, yet I felt good. I had never had any sexual experience or desires, nor ever had an orgasm, and I was almost seventeen. I was scared of Danno from my previous experience of him.

I once had a shower with Danno. He spoke with a soft, educated Dublin accent. 'Hold mine and I'll hold yours.' I have to admit that I did as he requested, for good reasons too. The last time I had refused to come to a lad's aid was my first meeting with the Brown Tango, and I was badly beaten up by him. What astonished me about this new guy was that he was a Jehovah's Witness. He never came near me again, though. I could not have pleased him, as I was still very naive in those matters. I realised I had to get out of this awful place.

Because of my toothache I stayed out of work for the first

time in the twelve months I was in the bakery. I went back to bed after my visit to the dentist, having had two or more teeth extracted, and I lay there listening to the sound of the traffic below my window in Middle Abbey Street. My face was out of shape and I felt alone and dumped, like a little boy in the woods.

I was gazing at the high ceiling when I heard heavy footsteps. It was my boss, Mick Bradley. I felt awful. Tears were never too far away; and as I write this I can still see the big man from Derry, so tall and straight, looking down at me; and his look said it all. 'I was concerned, Pat. You never miss work. Damn it, Pat, someone could have let us know. Pauline was very concerned, so I dropped in. The lads will be in later.' I just cried. I loved that big, affable man.

He pulled up an old green steel chair. He spoke quickly now, as though he wanted to go. 'Look, Pat, this is no fit place for a lad like you. I'll see to it you get a nice homely person to put you up, preferably in Fairview.'

Suddenly a few big lads entered the dormo, shouting. I recognised at once the loudest voice. It was Brown Tango. 'You sick or somethin', Collie?'

He stood a few feet from my boss. I just nodded. I hated the sight of him. Brown Tango got smart and shouted, 'Who's the big redneck, Collie?'

I responded, 'He's my boss.'

'I hope he's fuckin' payin' for you bein' out sick!' He came closer now, and the gang came with him. 'We'll have a nice warm shower together, Collie, perhaps when you're better. I need it badly.'

At that my boss stood up in front of Tango, who looked surprised at how tall he was. He backed off. Suddenly the caretaker appeared, shouting at the lads to get out and find a day's work and not be seen in the dormitory during the day.

Mick looked down at me. 'I'll have you out of here within a week, Pat. I'm glad I saw you like this.' As he left, I cried and smiled. I was happy.

A few days later I was on the move, thanks to Mick Bradley and his wife. Later in the bakery Mick gave me an address: 17 Cadogan Road, Fairview. After being told how close it was to the bakery, I couldn't wait to get there. As I went to leave that day, Pauline called me into the house. She began to advise me on how to behave, and told me that it would be a new start for me. She never asked me if I would like tea or something to eat: she was the sort of person who would simply prepare the food and put it in front of you. She had a lovely way about her, homely and caring: a real down-to-earth Dublin woman.

As I got up to leave, her words were most encouraging. 'You'll like the Mooneys. They're Dublin folk. Let me know how you get on, and if you have any problems come to me, Pat.' I was away on a hack to find my new home.

Number 17 Cadogan Road was only a few hundred yards from the Bradleys in Windsor Avenue, Fairview. As I entered the road I stood gazing down along the rows of red-brick terraced houses, with their six-foot front gardens all fenced off with neatly coloured painted gates and lace curtains in the windows. Number 17 had a cream-coloured door, with small panes of beautifully coloured leaded glass. The door opened and I was greeted by Mrs May Mooney. She hugged me and led me into the sitting room, saying, 'You're most welcome. You're home now, son.'

Mrs Mooney spoke with a nice soft Dublin accent and quickly made me feel at home, and I was treated like one of the family. She had one child, Lorcan, who was doing his finals in St Joseph's, Fairview. I shared a room with him, and he got so annoyed with my early rising that he once threw my alarm clock out the window. He hated the sound of loud ticking clocks in his bedroom – so did I. I had to find all sorts of hiding-places for the clock. Sometimes when it went off at half four I would have forgotten where I had hidden it.

I soon realised how different home life was from sleeping with over forty boys in a dormitory in the hostel or with two hundred boys in the dormitories in Artane, which still cast its deep shadow on me. But I also realised that I was out of my depth in the small terraced house. I found it difficult to relate to the family. The things I would talk about, I found they had no interest in whatsoever. At times I'd be told to shut up, though not aggressively, or unkindly. Lorcan often tried to help me change my ways but it had no real effect. I knew he meant well. And he was studying hard. He found less time to pay any attention to me. I suppose I annoyed people quite a bit in those days, yet Lorcan never really got angry with me. He regularly treated me to a one-and-one – fish and chips – for supper.

His father, Bill Mooney, was a tall, slim man. He liked his pint, and enjoyed it better when he shared one with my boss and the lads. Bill was to be seen quite a bit around the bakery, especially on a Sunday morning. I went to work on Sundays with Matt and Eddie, just for a few hours. I remember going up Windsor Avenue to the local shops and down Philipsburgh Avenue to the Pear Tree and along to Fairview Strand, delivering the pure hot buttermilk soda bread. Then I would be given a real Dublin fry-up by Mrs Bradley; it made Sunday work all the more special.

I began to enjoy life. The simple things pleased me most, like a walk in the park, which was only a hundred yards from the house. I enjoyed a game of football, hurling, or soccer. To these were added my new pastime of going to dances. The Irish Club became my favourite haunt; and I went to the

Theatre Royal on Sundays for my seat up in the gods. It was my joy, and I loved treating myself. On Sunday nights it was simply terrific to have your ticket and be one of the three thousand in the audience.

It was the custom to book a ticket for the cinemas on Sunday night; in fact, every cinema within two miles of the city centre would be booked out for Sunday nights. I was never one to be caught out without a ticket, as I could never have afforded to buy one on the black market. Cinema tickets were snapped up quickly by the black marketeers by midweek. But nothing has ever surpassed the Theatre Royal for pure entertainment; and no sooner was one show over than all I'd be talking and thinking about was booking for the next.

I began going out at night with lads I'd met in the Boys' Home but I soon realised that their company did not suit me at all. I was away from that system at last, and slowly I was beginning to change. I went to my first dance in the Irish Club in Parnell Square. I was awful with girls. I simply wanted to learn how to dance, and honestly I did not realise I could ask them out. I just believed they had to dance with me once I got up and asked them. Within a few weeks I was quite good at the old-time waltz, and I had the same partner I had begun with in the old-time waltz competition for the Mícheál O'Hehir Cup. It never dawned on me to ask my dance partner out. I had no idea about dating girls, or about sex for that matter.

I was still sleepwalking and having nightmares. I woke up in the wardrobe on several occasions, and other times I found my sheets and pillow on the gas cooker, while I was fast asleep downstairs in the bath. I often woke up fully dressed in bed, although I had taken off my clothes before getting in. I was wakened at three by Lorcan Mooney one morning with a crack of his shoe for shouting, 'Left, left, left right left! Lift them up, you pups, or you'll all face the wall!'

I was working very short hours in the little bakery. Approaching the end of my first year out of Artane, I believed I was on the road to nowhere in particular. The bakery business was not a great job to be in, working all hours or none at all. Bill Mooney decided to make a personal attempt to get me into the Bakers' Union. He had tried to explain to me why they could not accept Artane boys. 'You see, Pat, the bakers who work in Boland's, Johnston Mooney's, Kennedy's and O'Rourke's have all served their four years' apprenticeship. They then went to the tech in Kevin Street a number of days or nights each week until they were finished and got their papers.'

It was a father-to-son closed shop, just like Bill Mooney's job. He was a printing worker, and, as he told me, no one could gatecrash into the Printers' Union.

Bill read out a letter he had received from Mr Flanagan, the secretary of the Bakers' Union, expressing his sympathy with me and how he felt so sad for ex-Artaners, who were indeed well trained but, as I thought, undesirables.

My boss's business was in trouble, and I had been told I might have to go. Matt had already left. I went to see Mr Flanagan in the union on a number of occasions after that to plead my case, but to no avail. Then one day as I stood before Mr Flanagan, he looked me in the eye and declared that perhaps he could do something for me. It was a great relief to hear him say so.

'Well, Pat, I've got news for you.' I was delighted and relieved that I would not have to go to England. 'We are prepared to allow in a number of non-union lads like yourself who for various reasons did not serve their time under the auspices of the Bakers' Union' – in other words ex-Artaners.' I was thrilled, but only for a few moments, as he continued. 'There are two conditions. One is that you pay a fee to join the union.' Good, I thought. I couldn't wait to hear the other. 'The second one is that your father must be in the union and be a fully paid-up member.' I just laughed!

When I told Bill, he shrugged his square shoulders, smiled, and put his arm around me as though I were his son. 'Come on, son. Let's take a walk. I'll treat you to a one-and-one when we get to the chipper in Fairview.'

I walked home with Bill up the North Strand. Suddenly he said, 'I hope you don't mind me calling you son. If only May and I could have got you years ago we would have put you through St Joseph's School in Fairview.' I felt like crying, and wished to God he was my dad.

It was around this time, or shortly afterwards, that Bill began to explain the facts of life to me. We were together in the house and he had brought in a one-and-one. I could tell there was something on Bill's mind. Suddenly he said, 'Look, son, did the Brothers tell you anything about life: I mean the facts about babies, men and women – that sort of thing?'

I flushed and began to laugh. 'No, Bill, but I'd like to know.'

I watched anxiously as he lit up a Player's Drumhead cigarette. 'A pity May's not here. Look, son, it takes two to do it, know what I mean, like?'

I nodded to him, although I didn't really understand.

'You see, son, some women have lots o' kids. You might wonder why we have only one and some women can't have any at all, you know.' He was almost eating the cigarette at this stage. The small sitting room was wreathed in smoke. I was in bits. Suddenly he said, 'There are things you should know about girls, Pat.' Poor Bill looked awful; he was having a terrible time trying to come out with it. Then he splurted out the words, 'Intercourse, son,' when the door suddenly opened. He said hurriedly, 'Some other time, or perhaps the priest will explain to yeh in more detail than I could.'

I laughed at poor Bill. It was part of my nature to behave in that way.

I didn't realise then that Bill had his own problems. He never got around to finishing the conversation on life with me. It was some time after that that he told me he had to go away, but he never explained the reasons why. When I realised he was gone I wept, for I knew it was too short a while that I knew him. In that short time I loved him, and I realised that no one could ever replace him. To me he was a special man.

The Mooneys treated me as one of their own. May was a lovely person, as was Lorcan. I got on famously with him, even though I often disturbed his sleep. We never had a lot of money, but what we had we got great value for. I loved Dublin as a city. Being an ex-Artaner I suppose it was like being part of a great fair; it was smashing to walk home from the ballrooms without any fear of trouble. Dublin was a lovely place then. I hated going home too early in case I'd miss out on something, as I found the city at night to be a terrific place to be in.

9

In the year since I had left Artane, I hadn't changed much, as far as I could tell. It was about this time that I qualified with my old dance partner for the grand final of the Micheal O'Hehir Cup, to be held in the Irish Club in Parnell Square. I recall Lorcan Mooney asking me what I did when I was with girls. 'Well,' I responded, 'I love their company. I enjoy dancing and talking to them.'

Lorcan was quick off the mark. 'Is that all you do, Pat?'

I looked at him with some amusement and replied, 'That's all. What else is there?'

Minnie came to visit me at the bakery one day. I was very surprised to see him. He had grown taller; he looked like a real gentleman! We walked into the city, to the Palm Grove in O'Connell Street. The stories Minnie told me filled me with sadness. He too was a trained cook and baker. In Artane when I worked in the boys' refectory with him we were known as the kitcheners. Later I worked with him in the bakery, and he had moved on to work in the Brothers' refectory. Minnie was sent away to Salthill in Galway to a hotel, and then on to some farm as a houseboy. There he was very badly treated and abused, like so many other Artane boys, who were naive and had no one to turn to for help. I was lucky in that way: I was well treated by Mick and Pauline Bradley.

By the end of March a new baker had joined us. He was a rare one. His name was Mark, but he was known to us as Mando. He was tall, very dark in complexion, with deep dark-blue eyes and a round, handsome face. He was a slick talker and an elegant ballroom dancer. At that time we had a midnight start in the bakery, and I often came from a dance and went straight in to work.

I had got to know the people around Fairview and I was known in most if not all of the shops, especially those along Fairview Strand. The fruit and vegetable shop was run by Mr Warren, and next door to him were Jim and Peggy Behan, who had just moved in. Beside them was, and still is, Hogan's pharmacy. All these people lived on their premises, at the rear or upstairs. The snooker hall, which stands as good as ever, still backs on to the side of the bakery grounds and old house. Little has changed since, except that people have passed on.

In April 1959 I was in the old-time waltz final. My partner and I were quietly confident of bringing home the cup. On the night of the final the Irish Club was packed to capacity and the atmosphere was electric. My partner, who was training to be a nurse in the Mater Hospital, brought fifty screaming nurses with her. I believed we were going to win as the adjudicators moved about, casually eliminating couples. Finally it was down to the last six. I looked at my partner, who I had been dating just for the pleasure of dancing with her. In fact, at that time I had never actually dated a girl. I don't recall having that kind of interest, and I never had the urge to go any further than taking one step forward or two steps sideways. Yet I loved being in the company of girls, just for their companionship.

For the second-last heat of the final there was much more room to dance, so with the crowd cheering wildly I decided to take the floor by storm and walk away with the cup. My partner commented, 'It's between just a few of us now. It's in our grasp, Pat. My friends from the Mater will cheer us on.' I had never kissed a girl, but how I wanted to kiss her now!

To the cheers of her friends from the Mater, I put in some fancy footwork that Mando had taught me during our breaks. My partner and I were being cheered on by a chorus shouting our names, and I was about to say 'well done' to her when the music stopped. The hall fell silent on the completion of 'The Northern Lights of Old Aberdeen'. As my number was called out by the MC, the excited crowd cheered.

I moved forward when suddenly the MC announced that

number seven was eliminated, to the sound of fierce booing and catcalls. I stood there silently watching another couple collect the cup. Before I could gather my thoughts I realised that not only had I not won the coveted cup but I had also lost my fabulous dance partner. She slipped away into the crowd. I can only imagine how the poor girl felt.

The night to follow was to be a long and famous one. I had to dash straight to work. It was Eddie's night off, which never seemed to work out for us. Everything would go wrong.

One of the special virtues I learnt in school was always to be on time, that it was far better to arrive half an hour early for work or for an appointment than to come a few minutes late. I have followed that code all my life, and I'm not at all happy with people who turn up late for engagements.

I got off the bus in Fairview at Edge's Corner and I hurried up Windsor Avenue towards the bakery. As I entered the yard the church bell sounded. I noticed that the bakery lights were on as I entered, but I found myself alone. It was midnight. My instinct told me to check the ovens to see if Mando had forgotten to light them. There were two gas ovens, each of them with five decks. One of them the boss bought from Woolworth's bakery in Henry Street in 1957. I noticed that the taps were full on. I could see the light, so I decided to go and get changed.

As I was going, Mando walked in, his whites on and ready for work, but he said we'd be late starting because the ovens had only just been put on. Mando checked the ovens once more and asked me to go and get the supper.

I began to leave when he shouted, 'Paddy, get me the usual,' which was a one-and-one. When I came back and Mando had the tea brewing on the open gas ring on the floor. I could smell the hot plates heating up, but wondered about the ovens. I got the impression that something was wrong, and so did Mando. As he opened up the fish supper he shouted at me to check the ovens. I knelt down to check the lower deck, as from there I could see the jets and it was there I always put the light in. I shouted to Mando, 'They're out.'

After getting the box of matches, I glanced towards Mando, who was now sitting up at the table enjoying his chips. I bent down. I wasn't thinking of anything other than lighting the jets to get on with the work. I don't recall getting a strong smell of gas as I bent down and struck the match.

What an explosion! As I lifted my head up, the top metal door of the first deck blew over my head, and a ball of fire swept across the ceiling and scorched my hair. As I stooped down to get out of the fire the lower deck blew its door off, bashing my right hand. I ran out, screaming for help. I couldn't see Mando, but I remember the final explosion as

I stood or sat behind an evergreen bush in the front garden. A huge flame rose from the roof, and the windows blew out. As the ovens went up I could see a cloud of dust rise in Mr Warren's back yard. I'll never forget Mando's words as he stood in the front yard facing me. 'Me shaggin' supper! I was havin' me feckin' fish and chips, Paddy!'

I tried to laugh but I couldn't force it out, as my hand was too painful and I was in shock. I remember saying to him, 'Go and do something to put out the fire.' He looked at me with a grin on his handsome face and remarked dryly, 'I could do with a week or two off, Paddy.'

I staggered round to Mr Warren's shop. A crowd had gathered, wanting to see what had blown up. I was surrounded now. I could hear the bells of the approaching fire engines and was aware of flashing lights.

A man came out holding a glass. I heard his voice and recognised it as that of Mr Brennan, the friendly grocer. 'Drink this, me lad, quickly.' I was in another world, never thinking at all what was in the glass. Mr Brennan shouted again, as though I had been deafened by the explosion. I put the glass to my lips. I saw the golden glitter of the liquid as I gulped it down. 'It'll do yeh good,' a man shouted. 'Sure it'll do yeh no harm anyway,' said another. My eyes popped. The last thing I remember was Mr Warren asking, 'What yeh give him, Bill?' 'Glass o' brandy.' I was on my back on the pavement, looking up at the starry sky. The world was going round and round as I was lifted on to a stretcher and driven away at speed to Jervis Street Hospital.

The next day I was back in business, my forehead bandaged and right hand strapped up. I was standing in the bakery and looking out at the posse of policemen in the garden, searching for clues. I looked at Mando and we suddenly burst into laughter. The only clues I could see them finding were what Mando and I were to have had for our supper.

I was given a few days off. It was Friday and the men had hoped to get the bakery back in shape by Monday, to the dismay and annoyance of poor Mando. We began to move away from the bakery, to get out of the way of the gas workers – who had been blamed for causing the explosion, as they had been working on the mains up Windsor Avenue at the time. Suddenly Mando surprised me by saying, 'I need new lodgings in a hurry, Paddy. I believe you're well got in Fairview.' I smiled at him, not realising what sort of chap he really was, hiding behind his dark and handsome features.

I had left the Mooneys with much regret soon after Bill Mooney had gone away never to return again – I missed him dearly. I found Mando lodgings with my new landlady, Miss Cashin, who ran a small grocery shop beside the butcher's in Fairview.

She lived with her brothers, and their home was a real

throwback to a time more suited to a country village where Grace before and after meals was said aloud. The music was country and old-time Irish. *Songs our Fathers Loved* was played every night on the gramophone that was wound up by hand. The records were always seventy-eights. Each night after tea with the four lodgers, I sat by the open fire while they played cards and I embraced the emotional songs of Erin. I loved it. At times I grew so fond of Bridie Cashin, I often went to bed thinking she that loved me. I was accepted and it was a good feeling.

The Cashins' was like an open house, so many came to stay for dinner and remain on after a long night playing cards. Most of the men who came were famous Gaelic footballers who all played for their respective county teams. The old Irish songs that filled the smoky room often brought tears to my eyes of a longing for my Ireland. An Ireland free, an Ireland united north and south, an Ireland with four green fields, each one a jewel, each one free of British rule, just as the Christian Brothers had fostered into me. Yet I longed to be free, free to afford to travel to the land I was taught to hate.

England was evil, England was Satan's Island, even the English game of soccer was evil. The Christian Brothers sowed the seeds of fear of England into us as kids and yet I, even being very naive and gullible, was determined to travel and see the sights of London, Liverpool and Manchester.

Oxo, my old pal, had often talked about escaping to Liverpool to stay with his aunt. Often as I sat by the fire, as sparks flew from the logs, as the music filled and thrilled my heart, I thought of Oxo, the Burner, Jamjar, Stewie and my dear old pal Nick. They were all in England. My mind was on England. And 'tis there I must go, I thought.

I discovered I would need all my papers and a passport if I was to travel. I went to the custom house, and it was there I learned who my mother was. The details were bare:

Date of birth: 7/3/42
Name: Patrick Twoher
Place: Dublin
Mother's name: Helen Twoher
Father's name: Unknown

I was gobsmacked. But I was never to trace my routes for fear of what I'd find. My fear was I'd only find graves of the unknown.

10

When I look back on my past, 1959 brings happy memories. It was an eventful year.

I was settling into my new lodgings in 3 Fairview Strand with the Cashin family, who made me feel very welcome. This gave me a smashing feeling; I was really in my element with them. I was one of at least four lodgers in the house, which was fronted by a small grocer's shop, and beside it was Mulvey's butchers. Bridie Cashin ran the grocery shop. Sometimes I was asked to help out; the only problem was that I could never look straight at a customer, as I would get into fits of laughter at the size, shape or appearance of them – a throwback to my Artane days, when a new Brother was given a nickname within his first half-hour of duty. This was a real problem I had, and I was trying to change, as Mick Bradley had advised.

There was no shortage of things to do after work or at the weekends. Though there was no such thing as television or videos, I was never at a loss. Whatever was there we made terrific use of it. In one corner of the large sitting-room rested the old gramophone, which I fondly wound up by hand, and I sat back by the open turf fire at night listening to *Songs Our Fathers Loved*: 'The Rocks of Bawn', 'The Bold Fenian Men', 'Boolavogue', and 'The Rising of the Moon'.

I never felt alone in Bridie's place: there was a warm welcome waiting for everyone. It wasn't unusual for me to get into my single bed in the room I shared with two other lodgers only to waken up to find I was sharing my bed with some tall GAA county footballer, one of many such visitors to the Cashins' place.

I have fond memories of card games that went on into the night, while the seventy-eights on the gramophone kept the spirits high. I found great peace and joy just to sit and watch those men, all so contented together. There was no money to be won or lost, just good crack by the turf fire.

One night I heard a loud tapping on the window, everyone else being preoccupied with the cards in their possession. I answered the door; and standing before me, almost breath-less, was a very attractive young woman. 'I'm Isabelle,' she said. I stood staring at her, she was so beautiful. She was a few years older than me. She spoke again. 'Could you tell Terry I'm here? I hope I can stay the night. Is Bridie at home by any chance?' I could have fallen for her there and then. I smiled and said, 'I'll go and tell them you're here. They're playing cards.'

For the first time I experienced a sensual feeling for the opposite sex, and I loved it. As I sat down by the fire I couldn't take my eyes off Isabelle. What I'd give to have her take care of me! The more I studied Isabelle and Terry as they sat together by the fire facing me, the more I wanted to be in Terry's place. As I watched them I began to realise there was something missing in my life. Though I had no idea how to go about it, I began to feel I was spending far too much time with ex-Artaners rather than with girls. I wanted to be with someone like Isabelle.

I was over seventeen and – aside from my dancing partner – had never been out with a girl. Though I was really keen to try it out, I hadn't a clue how to go about it.

At the time of my first date I was earning £3 7s 6d a week and I was paying Bridie Cashin £1 15s for full board plus my laundry. I was in the happy position of being in the money, and I believed I could afford to chance going out with a girl, as Bridie often encouraged me to do.

Dancing was still my favourite pastime, and I loved the old-time waltz. One evening, while glancing through the evening paper, I noticed a competition being run in the Irish Club. I decided at once I was going. When I arrived I noticed a young, slim, fair-haired girl standing chatting to her friend.

The hall was quite empty, and as I approached her a chap got in ahead of me. I paused, and I was glad when I saw that he took her friend up to dance. The blonde turned to me with a really suggestive smile. That evening I danced in the arms of someone I longed for.

The competition was going well; we reached the quarter-finals. I'll never forget the great Gallowglass Ceili Band. They filled the air with their wonderful sound. I waltzed that night into the arms of love. I didn't have to ask her for a date, or if I could see her home. It was altogether different. We simply went together up the steps at the rear of the bandstand and had our Club Orange, eyeing each other, nice and easy. What amazed me about it was how simple it all was.

Noeleen was at least five feet six and slim, with blue eyes. Her fair hair was short and permed. She was nearly two years older than me, and she came from Drumcondra. With a little hindsight I'm certain if I had known just a little about sexual matters it would have worked out, as Noeleen was a joy to be with.

We left the ballroom together, though I felt I was following her, and wherever she chose to stop suited me fine. Whatever moves she made were new to me. I loved it, and was quite happy to go along with her, as I was on cloud nine.

We went for a lemonade and a chocolate queen cake at the small grocery shop opposite the cinema at the corner of

Dorset Street; it was a regular haunt for couples who went to the Teachers' Club or Granby Hall and the Irish Club. She walked into the laneway between the two blocks. We were standing in an old doorway, and as I looked across I could see the fluorescent lighting over the ballroom further along in Granby Lane.

But I couldn't be with Noeleen in the way she expected. She without doubt took the lead. I was nervous, to say the least. My arm rested around her shoulders. My hands were sweaty. Eventually I asked her about her last bus home. She smiled at me. She was so desirable, and was clearly attracted to me, but I was so naive, and I didn't wish to commit a mortal sin. I was constantly concerned about doing the right thing. 'You mustn't miss your bus,' I said.

Her hand took hold of mine and placed it inside her blouse on top of her breast. 'Never mind my bus, just feel my bust. Do you like that?' My body reacted with an unusual hunger, but I shook with fear of being seen. Then the sweat simply oozed from me.

I made my first date with Noeleen that night as I walked her to the bus stop. She stood at the stop and spoke to me in a way no one had ever spoken to me before. Her voice was sweet, soft as her body. 'Take me home. I've a lovely place. You'll love it. There's a laneway and a long driveway up to my house. There are lots of bushes.'

I felt out of my depth, and as I look back, perhaps I was out of my mind. I was concerned for her wellbeing and that she get her last bus, as I felt responsible for her.

Her voice suddenly became more seductive. She turned to face me. 'Are you feeling all right, Pat, here let me undo your tie and loosen your collar. Gosh, you are so tense.' Her soft, warm hands opened my tie, then reached to undo the shirt button.

I felt my body was on fire as she touched me but I froze as she pulled me to her. Our lips met, my heart raced, my mind was a blank. I couldn't begin to imagine how I could please Noeleen. I quite simply let her lead me wherever her incredible, tender, sensual touching found its way.

'You mustn't miss your bus,' I said eventually.

She gave me a very dejected look and said, 'You're not going to leave me here, are you?'

I felt embarrassed that I didn't know what to do to please her. Fact is I had no clue how to please a girl. Yet I felt I had done everything I could do to look after her. I bought her cakes and a bottle of orange. I'd seen her safely to her bus stop. I was certain that was all that she expected of me. I was really hoping she would understand, yet her awful expression left me in no doubt that she was utterly disappointed with me.

I began to walk slowly away. I glanced at my watch, and muttered, 'Gosh, I'm due in work in the bakery at midnight. Hell, I'll be late, I hate to be late.' Then I heard a voice calling me. 'Pat, wait for me.' I turned to see Noeleen dashing up to me, her eyes pleading. 'Please take me home. I've got a lovely house with a long front garden, with trees and evergreen bushes. My Mum and Dad will be in bed, please don't leave me like this.'

My heart almost stopped as I faced the first girl who ever had a real interest in me. Yet, I couldn't handle it. 'The bus is about to move off. The driver has started up the engine, you'd better hurry.'

'Can we meet again? You could get to know me better.'

How could I refuse her? 'Yes, yes, be glad to see you again.'

She drew real close to me by the bus. 'Next time you'll take me home. You won't regret it.'

She kissed me hungrily before taking a seat on the bus. Noeleen pulled open the window of the bus. She looked ravishing. 'I'll see you on Sunday night. Just say a place.'

Without thinking I said, 'Outside the Fairview Grand.'

She agreed. I hurried to get my bus to work, thrilled I had my first date. I was just seventeen and so naive.

I booked two seats for the Fairview Grand for the Sunday night showing. When I look back to that occasion years later, I realise that I should have booked for the city, the Royal perhaps, as she lived in Drumcondra and I in Fairview. What's more, I loved and adored the Westerns. I never even considered what Noeleen liked.

As we entered the cinema I headed for the centre seats. She pulled me back; I wondered whatever for. She spoke quickly as the lights went low. 'Follow me,' she whispered, and we ended up sitting close to the wall at the back. I turned to her and asked her if she liked cowboy films.

She whispered, 'No,' and smiled teasingly, her lips almost on mine. 'Do you?' I responded at once. 'Of course. That's the reason I came.' She didn't answer. 'Do you like Errol Flynn?' I asked her.

She smiled and shook her head. Suddenly she whispered, 'I like you a lot better. Are you really interested in all that horseshit?'

I laughed. A voice from behind said, 'Shush. Shush, please, or I will have yeh put out.'

After a while Noeleen whispered, 'Are you enjoying the film, Pat?'

I was glued to what was going on along the Sante Fe Trail. I didn't even look at her but said, 'Yes, yes, I am Noeleen.'

'That's too bad,' she muttered and suddenly she got up and walked out. Suddenly I was alone.

As I pulled open the bakery door the clock struck midnight. I was relieved I made it on time. 'How did your date go for yeh, Pat?'

I looked away from Mando as he took his fish and chips

out of the oven. I felt sick, tears rolled down my face over my lips. I could taste her lipstick.

'Your bleedin' crying, Paddy, did you screw her?' He laughed.

'I don't have a clue as to what you mean, "screw her". I didn't touch her.' Mando came up closer to me, his voice softer now. 'Look Paddy, did yeh shag her?'

I was confused by all of his expressions. 'I don't understand you, honestly I don't.' I felt gutted, sick.

'What did she do then, since you respected her and treated her so ladylike.'

'I don't know what you mean. I told you I treated her the only way I know, so what's wrong with that?'

He poured out the tea. 'Here have a few chips. I'll tell you what's bleedin' wrong with you, but first you tell me, did yeh take her home?'

'No,' I muttered.

'You telling me you had a date, your bleedin' first date, and she begged you to take her home?'

'No, no, she walked out on me. She's not coming back.'

He spilt his tea as he laughed at the news. 'Fuckin' hell, Paddy, that's an awful start for a first date. She walked out of the cinema on yeh, left yeh on yer own? You were naughty, weren't you, bit of a dark horse, surprise, surprise.' I blushed and was shocked at his suggestion. 'You're all red Paddy, there's no harm in that, after all, that's what they all yearn for, yeh know.'

I was disgusted with him. My voice was filled with anger now. 'Look, I swear to you I didn't put a hand on her. She kept asking me if I was enjoying the film. I told her I was.'

Mando laughed. 'I'm not surprised she fecked off and left yeh, you are supposed to please her Paddy, not ignore her. By the way, have yeh got a phone number for Noeleen by any chance?'

I wasn't thinking of why he'd asked me. I searched in my pockets. I looked at Mando, his dark beady eyes staring at me. 'No sorry, it must be in my lodgings.' 'What's that number written on the back of your hand?'

'Oh sorry, Mando, that's it.' His smile widened. His handsome face lit up. His voice softer now.

'Can I have it, would yeh mind? Perhaps I could help her.'

Suddenly my thoughts and fears of losing her for ever vanished. My hopes were high again. I gave him the number. He sighed, a long sigh. He seemed to be relieved. 'Good, thanks Paddy. I won't forget this. I'll do my best to please Noeleen for yeh. '

Gosh, I was delighted with Mando. I couldn't believe he was going to help her for me. 'What will you do?'

He looked at me cunningly. 'Ah, Paddy, gimme a bleedin' chance. I'd have to kill yeh if I told yeh that.'

I waited for him to light his half-smoked cigarette. After he exhaled, his gaze caught mine. 'Know what, Paddy,' he said, as he tapped out the butt of the cigarette, 'you're not of this world. Artane didn't just shatter your bleedin' dreams and wreck your childhood, it wrecked your bleedin' head, Paddy.'

'Are you really going to help me and explain to me what I do wrong when I'm out on a date?'

'You're bleedin' kiddin' me. Look, take my advice and give up going out with girls at least until you are a bit older, and learn a few things, get a bit of maturity, know what I mean, Paddy?'

'I'm not sure I do.'

'Well, that explains it, you are not ready for girls as free and attractive as Noeleen.'

I trusted Mando as a friend. I was a fool, too naive and gullible to see him as he really was, a chancer who was prepared to cheat and to lie to get whatever he wanted.

I couldn't get Noeleen out of my mind. I was certain I was in love with her, and with every girl that went out with me after that.

Looking back to those easygoing days of my late teens, in the late 1950s and fabulous 1960s, I can only laugh at how utterly gullible and incredibly naive I really was when it came to dating young women. So scared was I of committing mortal sin, I was quite simply too timid to venture too far in

pleasing or giving pleasure to girls I dated, such as beautiful
Noeleen. Though in truth, I hadn't a clue regarding sexual
matters, or indeed of the female anatomy. How to please a
woman was a mystery to me.

For eight tough years I had lived on a daily diet of constant
prayer and punishment. Fear of committing sinful acts in the
company of females was all due to my fears I harboured as an
orphan for eight years inside Artane. In Artane I had so many
reasons to fear committing sin, as the punishment was a
painful beating. Fear was the key to keeping the very strict
rigid brutal system in place, for the Christian Brothers to
keep strict control at all times of the boys' army of 900. The
system worked but ruined my childhood, and marked my
adult life.

11

As June approached, there was only one thing on my mind: my holiday, which I had saved very hard for.

At that time I was taking stick from everyone and for anything that went wrong in the bakery. Mando was the funny man with the dancing feet, and a smooth talker if ever there was one. He would simply borrow or beg to get any money he needed. He knew, as did others, that I had money saved. Mando would and did pawn the suit off his back, and anyone else's as well.

Mando was a slick mover. I found myself almost trapped in his company during 1959. He was in lodgings in the same house as me. I found working with him good fun, but being in the same house was a bit too much. Even though I had introduced him to the Cashins, I hoped he would leave.

On the first day he stayed in Cashins there were four lodgers at the table when the soup was served. Mando didn't think much of the soup, and while Miss Cashin was out in the kitchen he hurried up to the toilet with it, quickly flushed it away, and returned to join us. Miss Cashin came in to enquire if we had enjoyed the soup. Mando was first to answer, 'It was beautiful, ma'am,' and gave her a winning smile. I will always remember the look on his face when Bridie responded swiftly and poured him out a second helping of the soup. He never got the chance to flush it either.

Mando and our new van driver, Regan, were after the money I had saved to go to the Isle of Man. When Mick Bradley heard I was going by boat to the island he quickly offered to pay the airfare for me. I accepted, and was delighted. When Regan heard, he moved quickly to borrow fifteen pounds from me, and offered to drive me to the airport. What amazed me at the time was that men who were so mature and settled – some were married and had nice homes to go to after work – were begging and borrowing whatever money I had worked so hard to save. I never received any money back, as they had promised.

I fell in love with the Isle of Man the first moment I set foot on its soil. It reminded me of a paradise island in the sun that I had seen in the school cinema. I was overwhelmed by its beauty, its gardens, and most of all its beautiful glens. The names of Glen Mona, Glen Myra and Laxey Glen bring back fond and cherished memories.

I went alone to the island, but once there I seemed to find company without really looking for it. Perhaps it found me. I entered a waltz competition, and I had an English partner, from Redcar in the north of England. We did well on the dance floor, and I still treasure the photographs of the occasion. She was a good few years older than me, but nevertheless, I dated her, and it all helped me to enjoy the wonderful island. I sat in my room in the guesthouse, thinking that the English people were really human after all!

One breathtaking evening I was making my way up the steep climb known as Darby Hill when a young woman came alongside me, rather breathless. 'Have you the time, please?' I stopped, gave her the time, and thought nothing of it. A few moments later, nearer the brow of the hill, I heard her voice. As I turned to see who it was, she was upon me. 'Hey, Irish, we're going the same way. Mind if I walk with you?' She smiled warmly as the evening sun kissed her long golden hair.

'Call me Pat,' I said, and added, 'I'll be delighted to walk with you.'

She stroked back her hair and said, 'Call me Gloria. I come from Redcar, in England.' I was curious. 'Have you an older sister here?' She faced me and said, 'Yes, I have. She's in the dance championships.'

I loved the Isle of Man and the folk I met. England and its people filled my mind now! While I was away on my first holiday in the Isle of Man in the summer of 1959 I realised certain things about myself. These things were quite significant in my behaviour as a young adult. As I look back I can see that I was so inadequately prepared for life on the outside of the most feared Christian Brothers Boys' Industrial School in Ireland.

To be quite frank, prisoners in Mountjoy Jail would not have had to endure the hardship, the physical and sexual abuse and punishment we kids had to suffer every day of the week inside Artane, not more than two miles from the country's famous prison! It's very difficult for me to come to terms with this fact, that the country's criminals in prison were far better treated in their daily prison life than we Artane boys were in ours.

As an Artaner, I believed every word the Brothers said, as though it was the Gospel of the Lord. The hypocrisy was rampant: we were told that all sexual acts were a mortal sin; yet many of us were subjected to the most horrific sexual abuse. We institutionalised kids in their care simply feared breaking their laws, their rules.

Those in power, working for the Catholic-run state, the Free State Republic of Ireland, lied to me as an eight-year-old and they turned a blind eye to child sex abuse in their very own run schools and institutions. I and many thousands of other kids left these church- and state-run institutions poorly educated, inadequately prepared for life so far removed from their holy Catholic world of prayer and punishment where the mere mention of the word sex was strictly forbidden.

After eight years of Latin hymns, singing and devotions, I became institutionalised. It would take many years, very many in fact, to come to grips with the real world far removed from the one I was sentenced to as a child of eight. I could not come to terms with life in the real world, a world where women had their place alongside men, a world where men and women came together as one, as a couple, as a partnership, as lovers, as husband and wife. All I had been told was that sex was a mortal sin. Even thinking about it was a sin. Touching women was forbidden territory, along with touching your own body.

The trip to the Isle of Man in the beautiful summer of 1959 was the beginning of my realisation of just how institutionalised I had become, and just what Artane had done to me.

The Isle of Man was a great eye opener for me. I came in contact with many people from England, young people, and I found them all to be really nice, particularly the young lady from Redcar who danced with me in the competition in the Villa Marina. It was like being in another world: I just loved it.

I toured the island from Douglas to Glen Mona, Glen Allen and to Laxey. Sitting eating strawberries and cream in the Rushen Abbey, I just simply wanted this holiday to go on and on.

On a coach tour one beautiful evening the driver pulled into a lay-by and said, 'On your right, folks, you will see a cross, it is a grave and inscribed on the headstone are the words "Here lies the remains of some mother's son".' On the return journey I penned a long poem titled 'Some Mother's Son', after I'd heard the story from the coach driver of how and where the boy was found. On my flight home I harboured visions of travelling the world. I sure had itchy feet and I longed to see England and meet old school pals like Stevo and Oxo!

The Christian Brothers fostered a Republicanism and a hatred for England and all things English, particularly their sport, soccer. In their eyes, a game of soccer was a mortal sin and we were forbidden to play it – this rule was enforced with a brutal iron fist. Yet I harboured dreams of going to Old Trafford to see my hero Bobby Charlton and to visit as many soccer clubs as I could once I set foot in England.

I would return to the Isle of Man to work, and came back on many occasions to holiday there with my family. That first trip away from Ireland gave me a window on the world at large. It opened up my closed mind to the possibilities of travel. I was hooked.

12

In 1960 I was not getting anywhere in the bakery. I was losing my girlfriends as fast as I could find them.

In the lodgings I shared with Mando I was spotlessly clean – always dusting, polishing, and tidying up things that were out of place, forever putting things back and hanging up coats. I was very domesticated!

Mando was now the foreman of the small bakery, and I was his deputy. But it was not doing at all well. I realised that to get on I'd have to go abroad. I was becoming ambitious and I was no longer prepared to remain on low wages for ever. I was working all sorts of hours, which were very unsociable, and I began to get a burning desire to travel.

Mando came up with a plan of action. He told me on so many occasions how he knew England well. He wanted me to travel to Liverpool with him – a giant step for me to take. He told me that if I didn't like Liverpool he'd have me back without a bother. His plan was that he would take a week's sick leave and that I was to take a week off to simply try it. If it didn't work, he promised he'd have me home and back at work in a week.

On the boat journey to Holyhead, I listened to the playing of traditional music, as there were many fine young musicians and buskers on board that night. I watched many people with tears in their eyes seated uncomfortably on the floor or on suitcases. By the time I got on to the train I felt as though I had already been away for a week.

Mando knew all the ropes. I stood in the employment exchange with him. He had briefed me on how to answer their questions. As it worked out, I was given twice as much money as he was. We were sent to a big bakery outside the city; after a few days we were both given a sub – an advance on our wages. At last I had some real cash.

The house where we stayed was in a very run-down and dangerous area. Mando suddenly began to take a deeper interest in my wellbeing but, as always, with strings attached. He wanted my money for safe-keeping. Well, I knew my money was safer where it was – in my shoes.

One night Mando decided to retire to bed early. I was sitting up, listening to his advice and his new plans when suddenly the door burst open and two men stood in front of us. I froze. Mando jumped out of bed and realised that he was naked and his clothes were on a chair near the two intruders. The silence was broken when both of them roared with laughter, pointing at Mando. Mando shouted at me to give them something. Without even thinking I took Mando's coat from a chair and offered it to them. 'You want something? Please take it and leave us alone. We won't rat on you.' I was scared stiff, but decided to join them in their laughter. One of them came towards me and put out his hand. 'Shake, Irish. You're fun! You sure are some fun guy, I tell you.' I never took my eyes from him. I shook his hand and watched as the other chap moved towards Mando, who seemed to be frozen to the floor in the nude. Mando was suddenly being hugged by the guy. While he did all he could to cover himself up, the men hurried away.

On another occasion, it must have been four or five in the morning when I jumped out of the old double bed I shared with him. I was burning with a dreadful itch. I turned on the light and was horrified to see my body covered with bites and awful-looking lumps. I watched as Mando woke up shouting, 'Put off the fuckin' bleedin' light, for fuck's sake, Paddy! You're shagging blinding me.'

The next morning Mando got out of bed almost tearing at his flesh. 'I'm flea-bitten, for Christ's sake!' He was swearing like a raving lunatic now, and then he noticed that I was in an even worse state than himself.

*

It was our fifth day in Liverpool. Mando had had enough of the filthy lodgings, and I had told him I would rather go back on the boat than remain there one more night. I arranged to meet him in Lime Street Station, as he gave me a story about a business matter he had to attend to. He advised me to get on the London train before it was due to pull out if he didn't catch up with me. He would make the train, he assured me. And I, like a fool, believed him.

Well, I should have known Mando. I had a terrible experience on my first night in London – what I'd have given to have had Mando with me then!

Alone in a compartment on the way to London from Liverpool, I couldn't help but wonder where I would sleep that night. As the train finally eased into the station, I realised that I was totally alone for the first time in my life. I felt naked and utterly scared.

As I put down my suitcase on the pavement outside the station, someone asked, 'You waiting for someone?' The man who spoke to me had a smooth, posh-sounding voice and wore a nice fancy suit. I told him that I was alone and the man said, sympathetically, 'I'll put you up for the night and see you're okay in the morning.'

I thanked him at once and gladly got into his car. Within minutes I was in his flat. It was well appointed, and the lighting was soft and low, and very seductive. I was shown to a bedroom that had a large double bed in it and red curtains, which made the room feel very warm and luxurious. I had never seen such comforts before; comfort to me was sitting by the fire in Bridget Doyle's house in Barnacullia or in Bridie Cashin's place in Fairview, sitting by the open fire, listening to *Songs our Fathers Loved* on the gramophone.

The man introduced himself as Melvin, and asked me if I wanted a supper of tea and toast. I hadn't eaten for eight hours, and was very grateful for all the kindnesses he was showing me. Melvin called to me to get into bed and he would serve me supper there. It was a measure of how naive I was that I didn't think anything was unusual.

As I was getting undressed, Melvin appeared with the tea and toast, and I jumped into bed, embarrassed that I was almost naked. He placed the tray in front of me: buttered toast, strawberry jam, a pot of tea and two cups, and a tub of Vaseline. It never dawned on me to ask what the Vaseline was for.

Melvin quickly undressed and got into bed. I started to feel worried. It struck me that no one in the world knew where I was. I froze as he started to rub Vaseline all over my bottom. When he tried to penetrate me, I started to scream, and he quickly backed off. He explained to me that he had assumed that I knew what he wanted when he picked me up at the train station. Thankfully for me, he now realised that I had very little experience of the world, and he backed off.

The next morning I woke up to the smells of coffee, bacon and eggs. After we ate, Melvin dropped me off in Piccadilly, and his car sped away as soon as I closed the door. Once again I was alone, and I swore at Mando for leaving me the way he did.

I soon found myself at a bakery, Lyon's of Cadby Hall in Hammersmith, where I was hired on the spot to work six nights a week. They also recommended a boarding house for me. It was clean, had a nice view of London, and I found that I was settling in to work and my new life quite well. I even met Stewie at a dance in the Emerald Ballroom. He told me that he had found his parents and discovered that he had three fine sisters. I felt over the moon for him.

Stewie wasn't the only ex-Artaner I met. In fact, I was even working with one: Oxo, the great escape artist.

The first real contact I had with Oxo was early in February 1952 when I went to work in the refectory. Oxo had tried to escape many times, and had been caught many times. For that he was stripped and whipped with a long, hard leather until his bottom was raw and bleeding, or beaten on the soles of the feet, and had his head shaved, but instead of stopping him from leaving, it just made him more determined to escape.

I liked Oxo a lot – he took me under his wing when I arrived in the refectory. I admired his determination to escape from Artane, even though I never would have had the courage myself.

The day that Oxo escaped Artane for good, Stewie, the Burner and Jamjar staged a diversion by pretending to fight at tea one night. The fight instantly brought all nineteen divisions to their feet, and the noise of 900 boys stamping their hobnail boots on the rustic red-tiled floor and beating the table was overpowering. I prayed that Oxo would make it to London, and that I would see him there someday. I knew that if I had only half of Oxo's steely courage I also would have been scaling the walls to escape from Artane.

Oxo told me his story over many nights working in Lyon's bakery in London. He told me he had made his way to London after his last escape from Artane. As we sat in the bakery canteen night after night I listened to him reliving Artane. I began having nightmares again as we talked about marching to Mass at twenty to seven every morning, through hail and rain, and on to breakfast which consisted of a quarter of a loaf of bread, an ounce of margarine and a mug of tea. I wondered if a time would ever come when I would be able to forget Artane.

Oxo told me how, before he fled for good, he had escaped from Artane and gone home, only to be brought back by his own mother. 'Well, you see, after the first time I ran away, my Ma convinced me to go back, promising she would see to it that the Brothers would take it easy on me. She convinced me they would, so I went back with her. They promised her that they wouldn't hurt me, but once me Ma was gone, the bastards dragged me by the hair across the parade ground and let dozens of boys beat me. Then, as before, I was shaved and this time the bastards stripped me naked and sadistically flogged me. I could feel the blood run down my buttocks, down my legs, across my toes – the pain I suffered! You know, Paddy, I couldn't shit for a week after the beatings, my arse was so cut up. But I wasn't going to be bested, and when I got the chance, I scarpered.'

There was a real sense of sadness about him as he continued, 'The bastards never got me again. They taught us to hate England, but I got away, Paddy. I love England and what's more, the people here are more Christian than the Christian Brothers could ever be. Sure, they don't go to bloomin' Mass every morning, but so what?'

Oxo paused, and I could see the tears well up in his eyes as he told me that he couldn't forgive his mum for sending him to Artane in the first place, and sending him back after he escaped. 'I never returned home to me Ma and, what's more, I have not seen her since.'

*

In December I was feeling very homesick for Ireland, and working nights was starting to affect my health. One night I was at work when I felt peculiar. I was working on a huge travelling oven when I suddenly collapsed. I was taken to hospital, where I spent ten days. The doctors told me to give up the night work, and also the bakery trade. If only I could, I thought. While I was resting in hospital, I had plenty of time to think about what I needed to do next. London had been a hell of an experience, I was treated well at work and I was earning plenty of money. But I was longing to be in Dublin, in my own Ireland, in Bridie's place – sitting by the embers, soaking in the craic – and to find someone like Noeleen or Isabelle to communicate with. 'If only,' I thought. Meeting a girl was all desperately part of what I wanted. Finding her was one thing: holding on to her would be a real problem for many years to come because of my overpowering total lack of experience of dealing with the opposite sex. Yet I had an overriding burning desire to learn. I was over-anxious to please the girls whom I dated. I assumed I was doing okay, while of course they left me without me ever knowing what I'd done wrong. I had done nothing – perhaps that was my problem.

13

While I was in London I kept in touch with the Mooneys and the Cashins. One day I was sad to learn that Bridie was moving shop from Fairview Strand to Macken Street, near Westland Row. 'Blast,' I thought. 'There goes another good lodging house for me.' However, I was delighted to learn that I would be welcomed home for Christmas if I could make it. Well, I made certain I would, and I never looked forward to Christmas as I did then.

I had saved most of the money I earned while I worked in Lyon's of Cadby Hall, and by the time Christmas came I had saved a few hundred pounds. It was easy to earn good money then, and lodgings were cheap. I was working over sixty hours a week at night, which left me with little time for enjoyment. I quickly realised that machines had taken over from the skills of the baker. All the good was taken away by the fact that anyone could get a job in Cadby Hall as mere machine operators.

I came out of hospital about the twentieth of December. All I was concerned about was getting back to Dublin; and I was blessed to get a standby fare on an early morning flight when some passenger failed to turn up.

It was the homeliest Christmas I've ever had. The Cashins were to me what love and warmth were all about. While I was with them that Christmas I began to realise that it would be hard for me to stay away from Ireland for any length of time.

I was back working in the bakery that January. Eddie and Mando were also there. Mando explained to me why he left me in Liverpool, but I knew I'd never travel with him again. Eddie was about to leave to start a new bakery around the corner in Jim Behan's shop. Stranger things still were to happen. Matt returned to work with us. I always thought it was difficult for an ex-Artane lad to make the grade – always returning to their roots or the humble beginnings from where they began on leaving Artane. I got to like Matt much more now and began finally to understand him and his ways.

As I couldn't stay with the Cashins, I needed new lodgings for a few months before my travels. My boss Mick Bradley called me up to the house. 'I want you to take this basket of breads up to the Pear Tree, Pat. They're mighty fine folk and who knows, they might even be able to get you fixed up in new lodgings for a while.'

I made my way that Sunday morning up to the old grocer's

shop, the Pear Tree, and old Mrs Moore gave me an address. 'Molly will put you up, son. Tell her I sent you and don't you forget it.' As I turned to leave the colourful old grocer's shop, she called me in her loud southern accent. 'By the way, you make the best buttermilk bread I've ever tasted. God bless you, son.'

Molly kept a fine homely lodging house. Her home cooking and baking was one of her many fine features. She was a widow in her sixties, her family married and living all over the place from County Dublin to New York and one of her two sons was out in Australia.

Molly was a happy, talkative woman and enjoyed a good chat with her lodgers. She liked to keep to the back of the old red-bricked, two-storey house, spending most of her time in the kitchen.

The wireless was her one great companion and she rarely ever switched it off except when at night she retired to her room upstairs. Molly could often be heard saying the Rosary at eleven o'clock each night, a sure sign to any lodger who was home to tiptoe and keep quiet and a nice way of reminding us to say our prayers. I knew Molly found faith and strength in that way.

I felt really at home in Molly's house and I settled in very quickly, but my luck was soon to change.

I had just got in for tea when I heard a knock on the front door. I got up to answer it. When I pulled open the door I almost swallowed my tongue. I couldn't believe my eyes – my past had caught up with me. Brother Simon Davaro was standing on the doorstep. He sounded anxious. 'I was given this address. I was told I would get fixed up here.'

I was mesmerised, dumbfounded. He stared at me. I said eventually, 'Yes, sir please come in. I'll inform the landlady you are here.'

In shock I told Molly that a man had come to see about the rooms. Molly said, 'Tell him to sit down and to join you for tea. There is just the two of you and he can share your room. It is a double and you are only paying me for a single.'

I hurried back to finish my tea, not prepared to argue with her. I took my seat opposite Brother Davaro yet I found it too incredible to believe. I really thought I was imagining things as I sat facing a face from the past.

'Don't I know you from somewhere,' he said, as he placed his cup down gently on the saucer.

I stared at him for a long few seconds. 'Yes, you do Brother.'

He smiled when he realised I was a pupil of his. He reached out to shake hands and said, 'I'm Simon Davaro. Pleased to meet you again and in nicer surroundings too.' He smiled. I shook my head, still in disbelief.

I became silent and curious for the remainder of the

evening tea, not knowing what to say. I decided to remain silent and to let Simon tell me his story. He told me that he worked in the city centre for a semi-state body in a nine-to-five job. He was reasonably happy with his position in the office working for the company. But otherwise he was rather subdued. His mind was somewhere else, I guessed.

I feared his presence in the same house, and having to share my bedroom with this man. Not just any man, this was Brother Simon Davaro, an ex-Christian Brother, this was the Sting, Angel Face. It was very confusing for me – on one hand I liked him, but I was scared of him and of his past.

While he sipped his tea I studied him for a long moment. I hoped he hadn't come here to relive his past and off-load his experience upon me. 'I'll get more tea.' I stood up to go to the kitchen.

His voice was soft. 'Thank you, Pat. Your presence helps to make me feel at home, so to speak.' My mind went blank. I was shocked, in awe, and confused.

Molly was standing by the gas cooker, a half-smoked cigarette between her lips, rollers in her hair held in with a net. 'So you know each other, Pat. What's he like?'

'He was a Christian Brother in Artane, not so bad though.' I lifted up the teapot. Molly blew out a lungful of smoke. It clung like a cloud to the high ceiling.

'Are you scared of him, Pat?'

'No, not in the way I feared most of them in Artane.' But I am apprehensive, sort of scared of him I guess.

'He's a very good-looking man, Pat.' She faced me. 'Tell me, don't be scared. I can tell that you've been abused. It shows in you. I'd say they had boys like you, Pat, for pleasure. They had the power, Pat, they interfered with a good many boys, Pat. Am I right?'

Her gaze was fixed on me. I could tell she was reading my mind. 'Yes, ma'am, you're right. I better bring him in the tea,' I said, unsure of myself and what to say, or indeed how I should react, to this man from the dark, draconian past.

I was about to leave when she spoke again 'They were an anti evil shower of bastards, Pat, unchristian, a lot of 'em. I know a lot about them, Pat.' She tapped out the butt in the ashtray. Her gaze met mine, her smile was soft. 'Look, Pat, he's here with us. He won't harm you, I'll make sure of that. Any problem, come and tell me, okay?'

I thanked Molly and left with the pot of tea.

'Sorry it took so long,' I said as I poured his tea.

'That's okay, really. I'm used to waiting, Pat. I'm sure you know what I mean.'

I nodded in silent agreement. 'I'd love to have an office job like yours, going to work at nine o'clock and home at six, every weekend off, no night work. Could you help me to get a position like that?'

'To be honest, Pat, no. You'd need a degree. Without the education I'm afraid you'd be lost. I'm sorry to be so frank with you but it's true. You got no chance whatsoever of getting into the corporate jobs, or semi-state, such as the Civil Service, unless you got the education.'

'So I'm doomed to working in sheds in laneways or factory bakeries where machines do all the craft work and the bakers do all the physical labour manning them.'

'I'm real sorry, Pat, that we didn't educate you better than we did. I guess you had far too much work to do in the school bakery. Look, Pat, if you really feel you want to better yourself, for a better quality of life, you need to attend night school.'

What he suggested scared me deeply. I knew I could never go to night school. I had been locked inside Artane for eight years, eight long, hard years. I worked my back off from the age of nine years old in the kitchens and then in the bakery. I lived in fear of the Brothers in and outside of the classroom, of their leathers and their horrendous beatings. I had been scarred by my education; going back to school would never be an option for me.

At first sight Simon Davaro looked the real ladies' man and as far as I could see he was. But I knew there was more to Simon Davaro than met the eye. I could certainly understand the problems he was having. I knew because we shared the same problems born out of our time in Artane.

I still walked in my sleep. I still suffered from nightmares; I was forever on the run in my awful dreams. Artane still cast its shadow over me.

Simon was the same. Every night I would be awakened by him shouting in his sleep, 'Left, left, left right left, lift them up, you brats, or you'll face the wall.' Gradually his shouting and his talking in his sleep would die down without his opening an eye or waking up. Then suddenly the shouting would start again, much more pronounced. 'The wall, the wall, face the wall, hands above your head.'

Once, Molly knocked on our door to shout, 'You lads in there, are you okay or can I help?'

I got up to speak to her. 'I'm sorry, Molly, but he's having another nightmare.'

'Oh, the poor soul. Oh, what have they done to him! He's such a nice young man. Did he ever flog you, Pat?' She stared at me as though she already knew the answer.

'Yes, most of the Brothers used the leather – some more than others – but he never was like that. He was different, really, if you know what I mean.'

'Not really, Pat, they were all severe on the boys up there, I know, I've had quite a few ex-Artaners here you know. The poor orphans suffered a dreadful hammering, Pat, he could not have been all that different surely.'

I knew she had a point. 'Well, he did have to thrash lads and quite severely too, whenever he had to, I mean.' I wanted to talk about the sexual abuse, but I couldn't express my true feelings as in all truth I didn't even understand the real meaning of what had happened.

'Go on, tell me more,' she said.

After a long moment I continued. 'Simon was on duty each night in dormitory five. Once there he would have to deal with any boy put facing the wall, and someone always was.'

'You mean he'd have to flog boys day and night, you mean!' She looked shocked.

'Yes, morning, noon and night, really, and he would have had to deal with unruly boys in his classroom as well. Then he had additional duties to do. Being in charge on parade and out on walks, you see.'

Molly shook her head. Her expression was more sad than angry, I thought. 'Don't get me wrong, Molly, he was one of the best and he was always more humane, more real and down to earth. He was only hard when he had to be.'

Molly smiled, 'Of course, I understand. It must have been a hell for him as well as it was tough on the boys.' She paused, thinking for a moment. 'Poor lad, I feel he needs a good looking after, a good mothering is what he needs. God love him, Pat. He's living out his hell in his dreams.'

She put a hand beneath her right elbow, resting her right hand on her face. Her expression changed. 'You know, Pat, my son went to a Christian Brothers' school and received a kick in the ear from a very rough Brother. My son suffered deafness for several days after it. My husband, Lord have mercy on him, he would not hurt a fly. But he did go out there to see that brutal man and it was the only time in forty years of marriage I'd seen him so vexed. He took hold of that Brother by the collar. He had no fear of the collar that was around that Christian Brother's thick neck.'

I watched as Molly wiped her eyes. She looked at me, 'You are just as bad as he is, Pat, you walk and shout in your sleep. Poor Simon. He needs to see a doctor, he is that stressed out, the poor chap. Just as you do, Pat. You think I'm a fool, well, it's not only Simon's voice I hear at night, I've heard you too, Pat.'

It was a Saturday afternoon. The bright rays of the spring sunshine were beaming through the long Spanish lace curtains. I yawned. I felt tired. I had a late night and I was in no hurry to get up, but I'd have to make an effort, as at two o'clock I was to play a football match. I opened my eyes to find myself looking at the picture on the dresser of a beautiful woman. I hadn't seen it before; Simon must have placed it there while I slept. Her eyes were staring at me with a tempting melancholy smile. She looked radiant – such beauty, such elegance, I thought, and wondered how could I get a girl even half as pretty. I mused, feeling jealous of my roommate Simon.

I raised myself up off my single divan bed and stretched out my arms. Blasted stupid bakeries, I thought, as my shorts fell down. As I bent down to pull them up, I received a fierce smack across my bare arse. When I stood up I could see Simon in the mirror and his picture of his beautiful sister or his girlfriend staring out at me. I felt ashamed as I pulled up my underpants. I turned to face him. 'What was that one for?'

'The poor souls in Purgatory,' he said, smiling.

'I haven't seen you for some time. Is she your sister or what?' His eyes lit up as he lifted the framed picture. I was filled with curiosity. 'Is she really that beautiful?' I stared at him, then at the girl in the picture. He was taking his time to respond to my question.

'Laura Seymour, that's her name, Pat. She is tall, slim, very attractive, drives her own car. Her father is a businessman in the city. She has class, money, elegance, with a warm heart and a smile ...'

I didn't want to interrupt him. I wanted him to go on and on describing the girl in the picture. The girl of his dreams.

Then I thought of the time he desperately tried to force himself into me: I was only ten. It was hard to imagine he was the same man.

His voice was soft as he continued speaking. 'I shall never forget that hot summer's day by the sea in Clontarf when I first heard her voice. It was her voice that I first liked and her voice that won me over. Later, she drove up to Artane to see Marty, yes, she wanted to treat an orphan boy to a Sunday out. The more she came up to see young Marty, the more I saw of her and the more we saw of each other. There was no going back. I took off the collar and the cassock for her.'

Yet all the time he was speaking of his girl, visions of being held naked between his legs as a young boy raced across my mind. I was torn. I had always liked this Christian Brother, always preferred him to many others in Artane, but I could never forget that he too had used me for his pleasure, and that what he had done to me left scars just as deep in my mind as those by more brutal men, such as the Sheriff, the Macker and Hellfire.

Simon was keeping a very low profile while he was in the house, generally keeping to himself and rarely getting into long conversations with anyone. One evening, as I was in the kitchen with Molly, he knocked at the door. 'Who is it?' Molly called out. 'My hands are tied up in the pie.'

'It is me, Simon Davaro, to pay you.'

'Oh, come on through, Simon. Come in.'

He opened the door and smiled as he stood just inside the door, not knowing whether to take a seat or to say something. I was about to stand up and offer him mine when Molly pulled out a folding stool. 'Here now, put your weight on that now and rest yourself. I'll wet the tea shortly, son.'

It was still hard for me to believe that here I was, staying at the same lodgings as Angel Face.

Molly was bustling about. 'Just a wee moment now, Simon, till I put this apple pie in the oven. 'Tis for tomorrow's dinner, yeh see, and when the fresh cream goes on top of that, you'll soon know where yeh are, son, and where to put your feet.'

He smiled softly as he leaned against the old dresser, watching as she wiped her hands on her cotton pinafore apron, before pouring out two cups of tea. 'Now, Simon, young man, you help yourself to some homemade scones and buttermilk soda bread.'

Simon held out some money. 'Here you are. I owe you for a few weeks. I'll be leaving you in a few days or perhaps a bit earlier.' He made an effort to get up to leave. I could see she was surprised by the sudden news.

She looked at him. 'Sit down, you're not away already, sure ye've only just got here and what's more I've been meaning to have a long talk with you.'

Simon settled back down. Molly wiped her lips. 'Now Simon, I've been wanting to have a chat with you. I hope you don't take offence my saying this to you. I have been wakened up by you on several occasions, now, during the early hours since you came to stay with us, and by Patrick also, by the way.'

Simon looked embarrassed.

Molly stood with her back to the Aga, clutching a tea cloth in her hands. 'You know, you shout a great deal in your sleep, you give orders, weird sort of orders.'

'What do you mean, ma'am?' he asked with an extremely puzzled look on his handsome face. Simon became fidgety, raising his hand every so often to scratch his head or to wipe his sweaty brow. I could easily tell by his expression he was very, very embarrassed by it all. I felt so sorry for him, and remained silent throughout, knowing exactly how he felt.

Molly raised her tone. 'Look at me, Simon.' He faced her with a curious expression. 'Since you got here you have night-mares, very turbulent ones too, I might say. You keep shouting, "Left, left, left right left," and "Bend over, touch your toes, toe the line or you'll get six for the poor souls in Purgatory or Limbo" – all that sort of thing, as though you were in the army.' Molly turned her back and reached for a cigarette. As she turned again she drew on the Woodbine, keeping her eyes fixed on him. She pulled up a chair, exhaled and eased her heavy frame into it.

'Demons dressed as priests with sacred vows – child bashers, most of them. Sexually depraved child abusers, a lot of them Brothers were,' she muttered, then turned to face me. 'Do you agree, Pat?'

I was shocked. 'Oh, you mean me,' I spluttered.

'Yes, Pat, you, after all they put you through, son, go on, tell me.'

'Yes, I agree with all you said, Molly. The fact is Simon and I share in the same bleak past, we both have nightmares and walk and talk in our sleep, except I don't have a beautiful girlfriend like Simon does.'

Molly laughed. 'Very well put, you're nobody's fool, Pat. But you are a real survivor.'

Molly turned to Simon. 'I fear the road from here will rise up before you, it will indeed be a hard road that awaits you. I see by the picture on your dressing table that you have a girl.' He smiled, and nodded. 'So I'm right then. You must be planning to marry her some day.'

He nodded his head again. His tone was soft. 'Yes, very soon, ma'am.'

'Well it's a good thing we are havin' this little chat.' She reached for another Woodbine. 'God help the poor girl. You are not prepared for marriage, you need counselling, boy.'

Simon stood up. It was clear that he was embarrassed and didn't know what to say when confronted with his past. He made his way to the door, but stopped when Molly said, 'How soon do you intend to marry her?' I was shocked.

He held the door open. A look of surprise passed across his handsome features. 'A few weeks, perhaps. Well, actually the date has been set for some time now. I wanted to keep it quiet, you see. I think I'd like to go and relax in the lounge, before I go out. I'm meeting Laura at eight.'

She smiled for a brief moment. 'That's the kettle, Pat, you can wet the tea, son.'

I made the pot of tea as Simon went into the front living room. I really envied Simon; he had a beautiful girlfriend and I'd none. And this was the man who has caressed my naked body, who had masturbated himself against me.

As I left the room I heard his voice calling me, so I paused out in the long, narrow hallway just before I opened the front door. I turned slowly to face him. I was apprehensive, some-what scared of this man from the shadows of Artane. It sure was a long, dark shadow, I mused. 'You called me. Did you forget something?' I said.

'No, no, not at all. I was wondering, would you like to walk into town with me?' He paused, checking my reaction. 'If you are free, and you have nothing to do, that is.'

'But I thought you were meeting Laura.'

He came closer; his tall, slim figure, his good looks and charm would make any girl weak at the knees to hold him and embrace him, I thought. His tone was soft. He smiled a natural soft, easy smile.

'We've got a lot in common, Pat. I'm sure we can help each other. We could chat about many things that affect our lives.'

I was stunned by this.

He spoke again, more relaxed than before, I assumed. 'Are you free?'

I had pulled open the door. 'Yes. I was going out for a walk. I got no girlfriend. I can't seem to hold on to one.'

His smile lit up his handsome features. 'Walk with me into town, I'll introduce you to Laura.'

We walked in silence for a while.

'Molly is a very clever woman, don't you think?' Simon said eventually.

'Oh Molly, gosh, well, she knows all about your night-mares, Simon, and she knows quite a lot about the Christian Brothers as her son was badly affected and injured by one of 'em, you see?'

He glanced at me as we stepped out like two young soldiers. 'She really could hear me then, marching up and down in my sleep?'

'She did, Molly is no fool, Simon. Don't be put off by her

rollers in her hair and her easy-going style. She warned me about my sleepwalking and shouting in my sleep waking up the other lodgers. Two very nice young ladies left the house because of my sleepwalking. Molly told me I scared them half to death one night when I entered their room and crept into bed beside one of 'em.'

'You did not, get away. You tried to get into their bed?' Simon was gob-smacked at the news but seemed to enjoy it, I thought. 'Get away. You are so naive, Pat, so immature. You don't have a clue as to how you should treat a girl. I bet you believe in mortal sin, and just about everything you were scared into believing as a child in Artane School.'

I was shocked by him – stunned.

I stared out and down as far as I could see along the rail line going west, and longed to travel far, far away. 'Sure, you are right about me, Simon,' I said mournfully, feeling sorry for myself. 'But you know, Simon, I also know a great deal about you, and in many ways you are just like me. Sure, you are far better educated than I could ever be and you have a beautiful girlfriend who loves you. You are more mature and older and wiser than me, yes.'

He turned to me, his voice soft. 'So what are you getting at?'

'The fact is you walk in your sleep, talk in your sleep, you shout orders. Your bleedin' past will come back to haunt you and there is not a whole lot you can do to prevent her from knowing about you then, is there?'

I knew by his bleak expression that I had got to him and I felt relieved because he had it coming. It would help him once he realised who he really was and from where he came.

He paused again in the city centre near O'Connell Bridge. He faced me. 'Look, Pat,' he began softly, 'I love Laura and she has agreed I will marry her. I love her and Laura loves me too, Pat.'

I tried to congratulate him but the words would not come. I felt so depressed that I couldn't hold on to a girlfriend or to even please one.

After a long silent moment, the bells of Christchurch rang out eight hauntingly beautiful chimes. 'Here she comes, Pat, here comes Laura.'

I didn't wait to meet her. I quickly turned on my heels and walked away alone into the night, feeling lonely and deflated.

While I guess I should have been feeling happy for him, my gut feeling was it would be a marriage made in hell. Hell for beautiful Laura that is. Even I could see that Simon was no more prepared for married life than I was. As I made my way home to Molly's, her words struck me like a warning bell. 'But you do have awful nightmares, Simon. You shout and walk in your sleep, son. You are not ready for marriage surely. Does Laura know you well, Simon?' If only she did know the real ex-Christian Brother, Simon Davaro. If only she could have shared a bedroom with him for just a few weeks she would save herself from having to endure in marriage the nightmares and the horrors of Simon's past. Molly's words rang true.

I got home to my lodgings that night feeling sorry not just for Simon – knowing exactly what he was like – but for the beautiful girl in the picture on my dressing table. Laura deserved much better. I was pretty certain of that as I knew Simon Davaro much more personally than did beautiful Laura.

14

How can I forget the 1960s – the dancing years! Those were the days when we got super value for our few shillings. I was earning only £3 15s and handing over £2 5s a week for full board. But I could afford to bring my girlfriend to the Theatre Royal for a stage show and a film, have supper afterwards in the Palm Grove and pay the bus fares, and still have change.

Showbands were in huge demand in the late 1950s and through the 1960s. The National and Ierne Ballrooms in Parnell Square were very much the haunts of the flat-dwellers from the country and of north city Dubliners. I moved my Thursday dance night from the Irish Club to the Ierne, because I felt I needed a change and to try dancing to modern music. I met a girl on my first visit.

Noreen was to be my first real love, and when we told each other our feelings after only a few dates together, it was as though we should have simply gone off and got married.

Noreen was the same age as me, with long fair hair, blue eyes and slim build but with a sad face, suggesting that she might be lonely or homesick. I had only just met her but I believed we were meant for each other, as we had a great deal in common. Noreen came from a good-sized family in County Cavan. She had five brothers and seven sisters – and all fine girls too!

As I look back now I believe it is a mistake to linger and become undecided about what to do. If a couple have accepted each other in a loving way, then it's decision time. I went out with Noreen for many months and decided that I couldn't afford to marry her then – I'd have to go abroad to earn a decent wage first. I loved Noreen. I simply knew nothing of sex. I doubt that she did either. Nevertheless, instead of steadfastly standing by her, I got the boat to England like a fool.

I decided on my own that as I was not in a steady position that I liked – it was a dreadful source of bother to me that I was in night work and that I couldn't get a decent-paying, non-union bakery job – I would leave Ireland but keep in touch with Noreen. It never crossed my mind to ask Noreen what she thought. I suppose I didn't realise how Noreen really felt about me. I believed I was doing the right thing for the future. Now I believe it's wrong to put a love affair on ice, as I did – hoping to make a fortune somewhere and return to claim the girl you left behind, only to find her not there.

One night I'd been invited to Nulty Park House Golf Club by Noreen. I asked Lorcan along with his mother Mary. As we got ready to go out, Lorcan asked me about Noreen. 'What do you do when you're together, Pat? After all, I take it she's in love with you as well?' His tone was sincere and I could sense he meant what he asked, as though he really cared for me.

I noticed his mother listening now. I became embarrassed. I loved Noreen a great deal, possibly without showing it. I answered as best I could. 'Well, Lorcan, I simply do as she does. I tend to follow her, kissing, cuddling and that sort – know what I mean?'

'Is that all? Not try anything else?' He stared at me and then quickly glanced towards his mother as though waiting for a signal to go a step further.

Suddenly May spoke. 'Look, Pat, you've much to learn, and the sooner you do, the better. There's so much you can do with Noreen that will bind your love. I'll put you in touch with Father Tracy. He's very good at that sort of thing.'

I began to wonder what 'thing'? What else is there?

A few days later I sat in front of the priest, an elderly man. I couldn't wait to hear the good news about what Noreen and I were missing out on. I told him my confession. He quickly gave me my penance and shut over the tiny window. I knocked and he reappeared.

'Yes, son, what is it?'

I began to ask him in my own words. 'Well, Father, you see … I'm in love with this girl and I believe I should be doing things to make her happy and I've been told to come to you – that you know all about that sort of thing, Father.' I waited anxiously for his response.

Suddenly he blurted out, 'Whatever are you talking about, son? Who put you up to this?'

Good God, the sweat oozed out of me in the little dark confessional. 'Someone who knows you, Father.'

'Oh, I see – so they couldn't do it and they want me to explain it for you.' He paused. I could hear him sighing, and his breathing was heavy. He spoke quickly now. 'Do you interfere with each other's private parts?'

How could I tell him I felt her naked bottom while we kissed in close encounters, as my hands roved beneath her long skirt, but never any further. Nor did she touch me in that way. It was a very loving relationship without sex.

'Do you feel each other's bodies?'

'Yes, Father.'

'So you've committed mortal sin by your actions.' To cover his embarrassment, which was obvious, he added three decades of the Rosary to my penance, and the Stations of the Cross for good measure. 'Is she Catholic?' he asked.

My heart almost missed a beat. I answered, 'Yes, Father,' and waited.

He raised his voice. 'The Devil is in both of you, and as he always makes work for idle hands, I suggest both of you join your hands in prayer. I want to see you at the novena and sodality every month.'

I left the confessional none the wiser.

In 1961, after much deliberation, I knew in my heart and soul I had to go away, as I had no papers or diplomas to prove my skills as a baker. Although I loved Noreen, the desire to do well for myself came first. I will never forget the night I told her. She was ever so quiet. If only I had asked her how she felt! I was too full of self-importance, I suppose, always talking about doing the right thing. Though my ideas were good and made sense, I now believe I made the wrong decision.

My first port of call was Manchester. I kissed Noreen farewell and promised to send for her. As I sat up on the deck of the *Leinster* that night, my mind tossed and turned, and staring at the darkness of the sea all I could think of was my lovely Noreen. But I knew then I had to go on. My heart and mind ached for the one I left behind.

Once in Manchester I found digs, and couldn't wait for Saturday to go to Old Trafford to see my dream team, Manchester United, who were playing Burnley. After seeing the game I became a United fanatic. But I still had itchy feet, and I didn't like the digs or the city. The house I stayed in was in the district of Chorlton-cum-Hardy, near Medlock. It was a real Irish district. I shared a room with three young men from County Mayo. One of them, named PJ, was sitting in the room with me one day as he wrote a letter to his mother. He looked at me and said, 'It's hard to believe you're a Dublin man. You're so different really, and you haven't got a Dublin Jackeen accent.' I sat there listening, but my mind was on Noreen.

He tried again. 'You look homesick, Pat. What you need, boy, is a nice girlfriend. 'Twould be the best thing to settle you down.' I simply nodded at him, not knowing how to respond. Then he surprised me. 'You know, Pat, there's nothing better in life, and I mean it now, than spending the night with a lovely sweet girl – having sex with her. It's the most wonderful feeling you'll ever get, I promise.'

I sat there agreeing with him, and yet I couldn't relate to what he was saying. I was out of my depth, and I knew it. I thought about how experienced he was, and here I was, so gullible and naive. I began to think then that I was staying with all the wrong people. I knew I had to leave and move on.

After chatting to PJ I learnt about the islands of Guernsey and Jersey. I wasted no time, and booked a flight to Jersey. I was my own worst enemy, running scared, always packing my bags – on my way to somewhere, but it was really never important.

*

St Brelade's Bay, Jersey, in spring I can best describe as a semi-French tropical garden. I quickly fell in love with it. All that filled my mind as I wandered through the narrow cobbled streets of St Helier was, 'I must share this garden of beauty with Noreen.'

I found employment without any real problem as a baker-tablehand in the Sunshine Bakery in St Helier. I worked with a couple of old men, George and Alf; they told me no young people were interested in the trade because of the night work and long, unsociable hours. How right they were! But I was trapped. I was lonely and homesick and working like a slave far from home. But I was over-anxious to get on and make money.

I was going out to work at eleven at night and working harder than I had ever done since I left Artane. I was arriving back in my tiny bedsitter at seven or eight in the morning, yawning like someone who hadn't slept for a week. The best part of working nights was listening to the BBC Radio music hall shows. Radio was my great friend.

I knew I didn't look too good, and George and Alf were getting concerned for me. George, the older of the two, suggested I bring over my girlfriend. Old Alf, sitting up at the table and changing his false teeth to eat his supper, spoke very quickly, with a peculiar French accent. 'Every young man needs plenty of it.' Not even comprehending what it was I needed, I'd simply let his words wash over me while I thought of Noreen. Alf would continue: 'You know, Irish, you can't go on masturbating for ever, you know. You'll have to get your girl over here before you go blind.'

I worked with those two old-timers all through the dead of night in 1962, knowing full well how far behind I was in sexual matters. Crudity in the workplace and talk about sex confused and upset me. I knew I was one of the Brothers' boys: I felt I was better than those I worked with – which only helped to distance them from me. In reality I was no angel: I was simply short on experience.

I met Noreen at the airport. She hadn't changed a bit. 'What are you thinking about?' she asked shyly as I stood back to get a good look at her.

'Well, about you, of course. You still look the same – it's as though we were never apart.'

She seemed amused. Her voice was clear as always. 'You'd think you were away for years, the way you're going on.' She smiled and shook her head, as though she was confused. A bad start, I thought.

I began to dream of more pleasant things as I settled down to life in Jersey with Noreen nearby. No longer was I having nightmares or walking in my sleep. But I started to become anxious, fidgety and cranky in work and at home. I couldn't even please Noreen in the way she wished. I was always tired, and going to late-night dances at the weekends was out for me.

I was so naive I never once believed for a minute that Noreen would leave me. When she did, I took it as a joke and was overconfident by a mile, assuming that she'd come running back to me. I was sadly mistaken! I became very depressed and lonely, but as each day tore at my heart and mind I decided to tough it out, as I had been taught to by the Christian Brothers.

Lonely without Noreen by my side, I became a beach stroller along the golden sands of St Brelade's. I often meandered from noon until sunset. I dreaded the loneliness of my tiny bedsitter in the Market Street area of St Helier. I became exhausted from being up all night and beach strolling half the day. I lost a lot of weight, and missed Noreen dreadfully.

The summer of 1962 was a scorcher. I hated going out at night to work, and I was blaming the bakery and the long hours for all my problems. In reality, I was my own worst enemy.

I began to realise Noreen was really gone. My first love. Whatever love she had for me suddenly evaporated when she settled in Jersey. My heart ached. My pride hurt beyond repair. I found it almost impossible to come to terms with the suddenness of how I lost her. Nor could I quite comprehend what I'd done to make her leave me in this way. The truth is, I had done nothing. I was so fearful of committing a sinful act. Being so naive, I failed to satisfy and please her. I had done nothing to abate her hunger and passion that could have bound our love. I guess that was the core of my problem back then.

I realised there was something strange about the way I related to girls, but the gulf I was desperately trying to bridge only seemed to get wider. Often I was left with the feeling that if only I had tried to be normal and forget about my high principles, or if only I had tried not to distance myself from them and just go out with them without falling in love too soon, it would have been all right. I was far too naive to please girls, treating them kindly but often with far too much delicacy.

As the season wore steadily on, I was becoming exhausted, having been working up to seventy hours a week, six nights a week. While still hoping for Noreen to come back to me, I took a trip out to St Brelade's Bay one hot Saturday afternoon in August. The weather and the atmosphere were beautiful.

Then I saw Noreen. She was strolling along the hot sands of the bay with a boyfriend, their arms around each other, two beautiful lovers. My heart sank to a new low, and I was in tears. Then, like a soldier, I stepped it out, and went for a walk along the country roads.

As I made my way along a narrow country lane, I was sure I had heard a cry for help. I looked about, waited, then a second cry. There was a low hedge, and I hurried towards it, past what looked like a mansion – a big farmhouse, I guessed at a glance. I noticed a bicycle lying over the ditch, and beside it a young woman in some distress.

My depression vanished as I offered to help her.

'Thank you.' She smiled up at me and added, 'I've got a punctured tyre and hurt shoulder. Please can you fix it for me?' I was thrilled to be of some help. When she spoke again I fell in love with her French accent, and the way she smiled helped to erase any thoughts of Noreen.

'I'm Maria Duvarre. I live next to that farmhouse, where I work as an au pair. The family are away. I'm alone.'

I introduced myself, and fell over the scooter. 'Damn it,' I said. I looked up at her, she was so beautiful.

With a neat flick of her hand she brushed back her long auburn hair and laughed loudly as I lay across it. 'Oh, you Irish, you are funny people.' I hadn't told her I was Irish.

Having repaired the puncture for her, I was dripping with sweat. As I stood gazing about, wondering where I could wash myself, I heard her voice calling, 'Pat-rick, Pat-rick, please come and you have shower. You are so dirty and hot.'

While I was working on her tyre, she must have slipped off. I looked about to see where she was, and there she was, up on the balcony of the big stone farmhouse, dressed in a bathrobe. My heart missed a beat. No more 'if onlys', I hoped. My time had come at last.

I entered the huge house. Maria appeared. I became flushed as she stood in her pink bathrobe, gesturing to me to come up. 'Now you need to shower, Pat-rick – perhaps then we have a drink. You Irish love your drink.' She smiled at me, but little did she realise that I never drank alcohol.

I was shocked as she got under the shower with me. This time I was determined to go along with Maria to please her but also, more important to me, for the experience. It's now or never, I thought. It was as if I was in a state of complete paralysis beneath the shower as her body touched mine. Then we passionately caressed each other while the cool water flowed down on us.

She held the glasses of sparkling champagne and placed the bottle on the floor. She held a glass up to me and as I took hold of it, we touched glasses. A beautiful feeling came over me. I was always a fast drinker – of tea, that is – and no sooner had I downed my first than she filled it again. For the first time I realised I was intoxicated. I closed my eyes for a silent moment. 'I'll have a lot to confess next time,' I muttered. 'But nothing can stop me, now.'

Maria looked at me with a smile. 'You speak, Pat-rick? Tell me, I like you very much, so you make me very happy.'

I must be doing something right, as Maria was so happy and contented. I couldn't get myself to express fully how wonderful I felt. This was a joyful new experience for me.

'You need towel, Irish. It's here. Come, you'll see. Hope you don't mind me call you Irish, Pat-rick.'

Maria was waiting in the open door with a long bath towel. I could taste the breathtaking sweetness of her fragrance as she began to towel me down. What am I to do? I wondered to myself. Just let it happen.

She led me into her room and slowly fell backwards on to the huge old bed with a velvet canopy, pulling me with her. For a while I felt I was lying beneath a chapel dome, though in reality I was on top of beautiful Maria. I was hoping Maria would lead the way; the last thing I wanted now was for me to mess it all up and be left feeling sorry for myself.

I felt Maria's fingers dig deep into my flesh, her mouth on mine. What do I do now? I wanted her to help me, because I didn't know what to do.

Then Maria gently took hold of me, and I experienced the ecstasy of love. Afterwards, as I lay on my back, a dreadful thought struck me: I'd committed a mortal sin – but at least I was normal. I'll confess later, I thought.

Maria reached for the wine glasses. She smiled as she handed me a full glass and said, 'You make me so happy. It was so good. I'd love to have you to stay whole night but I'm not allowed to have friends after eleven o'clock at night. See, I must go by the rules of this house, okay, Pat-rick?'

I wanted to remain in this fragrant garden for as long as my heart beat.

The room grew darker. I must have dozed off. It was time to go. I gazed down at Maria as I said my goodbyes. 'I will never forget you, Irish.' She paused for a brief moment, smiled, and said, '*Au revoir*, Pat-rick, thank you for fixing my tyre.'

As I left Maria, in her perfumed French garden, I suddenly felt sad as I realised that I'd never see her again. Her beautiful naked slim French body was now imprinted on my mind.

As I marched along the narrow road by many such farm-steads and beautiful homes, as the sun lowered to kiss the calm blue water of St Brelade's Bay, I wondered where I could meet another beautiful French au pair and be so lucky as to enjoy a loving cool shower with her. To experience the gentle-ness and softness of her French touch, to embrace the sensual warmth of her body so eager to be pleased. I longed to meet another Maria.

15

In October I was back home in Fairview, working for James Behan in the bakery in Fairview Strand, and once again I was in lodgings with the Mooneys in Cadogan Road.

While I was playing soccer in Fairview Park one Saturday with a few ex-Artane lads and a team from Fairview, there was a schools hurling match on the pitch beside us. I had noticed the Drisco, who I worked under as a cook and a kitchener in Artane, and also a few other Christian Brothers; but the one who got most of my attention was the Macker. That Brother looked every bit as tall and as hard as the time he battered my best pal, Minnie, around the head and face with his open hands until he told him where he had hidden a pencil in the dormitory. Poor Minnie gave in. The silly pencil was found in a flower pot on the window ledge, and the next morning poor Minnie was practically unrecognisable.

I was close to the Macker as he stood on the sideline watching the team when suddenly I heard him call me, using my Artane nickname, Collie. I walked up to him. 'You called me, sir?' I stood looking up at the man who so often beat me with his dreadful leather for such silly things as being caught out of bed swapping a *Dandy* or a *Beano* with a lad a few beds away. I had quaked with fear of that tall Christian Brother whenever he was in charge of our dormitory: fear of wetting my bed and of being flogged by him for it. He slowly reached his right hand into an inside pocket and pulled out a wallet. He spoke quickly and smiled as he did so. 'I've got something to show you, Collie. Do they still call you that?'

'No, sir, not now. They call me Paddy or Pat now.'

I watched him open the wallet and take out an envelope. 'I've got a picture of you, Pat, and a few of your pals from Barnacullia.' He handed them to me.

'But it's me, sir, making my Confirmation, and one of my pals too. How did you keep them so good, sir, for so long?'

I looked again at them. I noticed all the lads who were in my class that year, back in 1954. He suddenly handed me the envelope and said, 'Keep them, Collie. I've had them long enough now. I suspect you're keeping well and out of trouble, as so many have problems, you know. Keep up your prayers and go to Mass.' He turned and walked away.

Though I was shocked, I suddenly felt a tinge of sadness for this cruel and brutal Christian Brother. It's so difficult to harbour revenge and hatred for so long. In many ways I'm sure he had regrets for being so cruel and evil towards so many boys in care, as he was to my pal Minnie and me. Time takes care of all our sorrows and heals our wounds, I thought, as he went on his way. In many ways he reminded me of Simon Davaro. The shadow of Artane haunts them all, I mused.

I met that Brother several times after that, riding his bike through Fairview, and he always stopped and chatted to me, always giving me sound advice. After each occasion we met I understood more of the man and the fact that the shadow of Artane had left its mark on him also. It struck me then that it is never too late to change.

At the turn of 1963 things were not really working out in Home Bakery. I found working with some of the lads a bit too much. The wages were awfully low: four pounds ten shillings. I told Jim I would have to leave if he couldn't give me a rise of at least ten bob – 50p. In response he drew out a right, and I hit the floor. After a punch-up we ended up shaking hands in Clontarf Garda station; and I did get a small increase after that.

From 1960 to 1968 I seemed to be working between Ireland, England and Jersey. I got that bug about working in Jersey for the summer season. Each time I'd return to Dublin

I would stay with one of my old landladies. I went back to the Mooneys in Fairview quite a lot.

While waiting at Dublin Airport for my flight to Jersey, I came face to face with my former drill master, better known as Driller the Killer. With him was none other than the famous Brother nicknamed the Hellfire, dressed in casual clothes. As I sat down and waited for my flight number to be called, I thought of those two Christian men.

Hellfire, who taught me for two years, got his nickname from producing pictures of Hell and scaring the children in the classroom with them. He beat boys' naked buttocks so badly that the blood seeped through their shorts. He often made me stand out facing the wall with my hands held above my head for long periods; if I let my hands drop, he would beat the legs off me. Driller the Killer was no ordinary drill instructor. He beat lads so badly that they were often removed to hospital or to the infirmary. Some lads never returned.

Summer of 1967 was special. I met up with Helen, a lass from Bingley in Yorkshire, at a dance. Helen was light on her feet, the music was old-time and we danced until the music died. Every moment with Helen was simply wonderful. I quite easily fell in love with her as we walked home to her apartment by moonlight to the sound of the tide lapping and slapping over the rocks in Grave de Lec. I was floating like a piece of driftwood on a moonlit bay as I entered her apartment.

'Make yourself comfy,' she said. 'Take your coat off. Tea or coffee?'

'Tea. Thank you.'

As I looked about I noticed piles of children's homework. So Helen was a teacher. Her voice rang out. I loved her accent. 'Do you like toasted ham and cheese?'

'Yes, thank you.'

'It's on the table. Come and get it. You can tell me all about yourself then.'

I gazed at her as I drank the hot, sweet tea. She was so chatty and cheerful while I became slow and somewhat overwhelmed by her. 'So what's your full name then?'

I began, 'I'm Patrick.'

'You told me you were Larry at the dance.' She seemed to be surprised.

'Laurence is my middle name and I'm known as Larry at work. You see, they have one chap who is called Paddy and one Pat.'

'Ah, that explains it then. I much prefer Larry anyway. So you are a baker, then?'

I nodded, 'Yes.'

'More tea then, or do you prefer red wine perhaps?'

I couldn't tell her I was a teetotaller. I took the glass of wine. I felt relaxed in her company, though she always took the lead. As I sipped the red wine I realised we had many things in common: her passion for drama, music and travel and, by the time the bottle of Merlot lay empty on the floor, her passion, drive and hunger for love.

For weeks that hot summer we walked miles along the golden sands of St Quans and St Brelade's Bay. It was odd, but because we were together all the time I never thought to get her phone number. One evening we strolled along the sandy beach at St Quans, not far from West End Park where I was soon to start a new nine-to-five job. I could tell that she had something to say to me. 'What's on your mind, Helen?' I felt anxious, while I waited for her answer. There was a strange pain in my forehead and my back ached.

'I'm going to Australia with my best friend, Gloria. She's from Bolton, Larry, and we're both going to teach there. We got it all sorted out. The school is in New South Wales.'

'When? How soon?' I held her. As she gave me the details, I muttered, 'December, my God. When do you leave Jersey?'

'September. I will be at home in Bingley. You can come and visit me there if you want.'

'Are you sure?' My foolish heart. I was sorry I said that.

'Of course I'm sure. Don't you trust me? I'd love you to come to my home in Bingley. It's Yorkshire for me, Larry, and New South Wales for Christmas. What will you do?'

'Go back home, I suppose.' I felt gutted. 'No, I got no place to go home to, Helen.'

'Oh goodness, Larry. I'm so sorry. I mean it. Come to Australia with us. Think about it.'

'I'm fine. It's the darn night work and lack of sleep, that's all.'

As we parted, Helen said, 'You've got my address in Bingley. Write to me. I'll let you know when you can come visit me and you will think about coming to Australia, won't you? Promise me.'

I promised I would. But she was right about me not looking so well.

I began in my new job at the beginning of August and I was feeling just awful. I decided to visit the hospital near West End in St Helier.

The tall, well-built, heavy-set doctor addressed me in a thick Scottish accent. 'Can I help yeh, laddie? What have you come here for?' His tone was gruff.

'I think I got maybe a flu. My head aches awful.'

He stood towering over me, his tone as rough as Scottish haggis. 'You'll live, laddie. All you Irish and English who come in here with summer colds think yer dying. Now clear off, I mean it, and do a good hard day's work, lad.'

I was stunned to silence and I felt embarrassed. I walked back to the flat that I shared with a man called Billy from Dundee and an English lad, feeling light-headed.

A few days passed. It was about four o'clock in the morning. Billy heard my groans for help but he fell back to sleep. He was fond of Scotch whisky. I felt I was dying as I found it so difficult to breathe. The time was nearer 4am. I couldn't lift my head off the pillow. My head ached. I moaned. Then the English lad muttered, 'Go to the doctor, Larry, or go to the hospital first thing. Now get some sleep.'

I just closed my eyes as any bit of light affected me. The hours dragged on like days. I tried to pray to God for forgiveness for all my sins I was sure I'd committed with Helen, as even thinking about her nakedness, of her breathtaking body, is a mortal sin. I felt scared to die in a state of mortal sin, yet I couldn't get those thoughts out of my mind. I was moaning when I heard a voice with an English accent. 'Here, Larry, take these and drink this.' My flatmate lifted my head up as I took the painkillers. 'Drink all the water, Larry. You got the flu. Now try to sleep.'

The next day I was able to get up. I decided to go to the chemist along the main road. I felt strange to be in the sunlight. It hurt. I remember entering the chemist. The staff wore white coats. My gaze rested on a young, dark-haired female assistant who approached me. 'Can I help you at all?'

I remember her brown eyes searching me. Her voice was more anxious than before. 'Gosh, let me help you. Come this way, please. You are not well. We got a doctor upstairs. She will see to you.'

How I felt the burden of each step. I felt the nurse's arms around me. I heard a female voice.

'I'm going to take your temperature. Pulse low, temperature, goodness, 105. Doctor, doctor.' Her tone was anxious. 'Call the ambulance. Say it's most urgent.'

The doctor asked, 'Are you here alone?'

I mumbled yes.

'Got a name? Try to whisper it to me. Please try.'

I managed to give the doctor some details.

'How long have you been feeling this way? Please take your time. A week. I see. Been to see a doctor, have you?'

I nodded yes, in hospital, and blurted, 'He's Scottish. A big man.'

I felt her hand holding mine. 'You've done fine. Say no more now. We know the one you mean.' I heard the siren. It must be outside, I thought.

In the hospital I was naked, surrounded by a team of male and female doctors and nurses. I screamed in agony as they probed a long needle up into my lower back for fluid. The pain was horrendous. 'We got it, lads. We got it. Get it to the lab. It's an emergency.'

Later that night I lay naked as nurses cooled me down with ice-cold towels. The doctor came by, on his round, I guess. 'How is he, nurse?' God, it's him. It's the big Scot who told me to get out. I was surrounded by the team in white coats.

As I lay flat on my back, my eyes unable to face the light, I listened to the nurse give my details to the big Scots doctor and the team. 'Temperature slightly improved, 103. Pulse flow same. Remains feverish, can't face light.'

'Okay, nurse. Let me get a closer look at him,' said the doctor. His tone was much more polite. He was very apologetic too. 'Well, we meet again, Patrick. But I promise you we are going to take very special care of you this time. 'You're overheating, lad. Too much sun. You've got a severe form of viral meningitis, Patrick. When we get you back up and out, you must promise me you will keep out of the sun. It does not agree with you. Take good care of him, nurse. Minimum visitors, one at a time, and give them protective clothing and masks. No lights, keep the blinds closed. Plenty of water. Expect he'll be with us for a long stay. I'll see you tomorrow, Patrick.'

I heard the team walk out, the door closed. The sounds hurt my head. How I longed to see Helen now. I felt so weak. I couldn't lift my head from the pillow or open my eyes to see the daylight. I received one visit during that time from my friend Billy. He told me that he would try to find Helen for me, but that was the last I ever saw of him.

A few weeks later the Scottish doctor came to give me good news. 'You are on the mend, laddie, you are going to learn to walk again, and you will get to see the northern lights of old Aberdeen, I promise you. It's 105 degrees outside, the hottest August on record. Aren't you lucky you are out of the sun in here in the shade, with a team of pretty nurses taking care of you.' He squeezed my hand in his and said, 'I prayed every day and night for you.'

'A prayer for you too, doctor.' I had come to admire this man, and I was deeply moved by his words of kindess. 'I would love to see Aberdeen.'

'In the gold of October,' he said. I nodded in agreement.

I will go there, I thought.

Once I was able to stand up without support from the kind, caring nurses, I slowly became strong enough to walk the long, polished corridors. Nurse April, a dark-haired young lady who was on duty to escort me up and down the stairs, helped me to get strength back into my legs and was there for me in the days when I felt I had no desire to live. I'm certain I would not have survived without her special gentle care. She was my angel.

It was a beautiful golden day in early September. I was building up my strength walking along the white sandy beach when I heard a voice calling. 'Larry, Larry.' My heart stopped briefly as I turned around. 'It's me, Gloria, Helen's friend.'

'Where is she?' I felt so emotionally drained. I just wished she would embrace me. I wasn't disappointed.

'She's gone home to Bingley. She left a get-well card. We heard far too late about your awful illness and your close shave with death. When we got the news we both cried,' she blurted out.

Gloria withdrew Helen's card from her shoulder bag. As I read it, I smiled. My heartbeat raced.

'Good news, Larry?'

'Yeah, Helen would like me to stay a few days in Bingley once I'm fit enough.'

'That's a nice surprise after all you've been through. You know Helen and I are off to Australia in December.'

After a long pause I said, 'Yes I do. But I guess it would be far too hot a climate for me. I'm off to Aberdeen soon.'

We walked for miles as we chatted about Bolton, Bingley, Shipley and Aberdeen. She was so much taller than Helen and she spoke so clear. A school teacher to the tip of her fingertips, I thought.

*

After I was discharged from hospital, I did go to Aberdeen as I had promised the doctor. There I found work and also met a girl, Sarah, whose family seemed to be planning our wedding after two weeks. I liked her, but she was no Maria or Helen. I was a non-drinker and non-smoker, while she smoked like an old chimney and drank her Scotch the way I drank tea. And then when I'd tried to kiss her she smacked me, and this was when she was sober. I feared what she'd do after a few drams too many!

It wasn't long before I contacted Helen and I was on the next train to Bradford. Our agreed meeting place was on the bridge in Bingley town over the River Aire and as I stepped from the Bradford–Bingley bus my heart missed a beat. As she embraced me, I could not stop the flow of tears and emotional joy that overwhelmed me. When she released her hold, her eyes met mine. Her tone was soft and wavering. 'Oh, Larry, forgive me for not getting to see you in hospital when I heard of how close to the end you were, but I had left for home then. Gloria told me all about how you almost died. Oh God, Larry, if only I'd known I'd have been there for you. I cried so much when Gloria phoned me. In fact we both did. She told me everything. I want you to know I really loved you then.'

My hopes raised. 'And what about now?' I said.

'Oh, Larry, I'm so fond of you. I had to see you again after all you've been through but you know I'm going to Australia.'

As we strolled along the mossy green banks, I listened to her explain her plans in New South Wales and how she had dreams of going to Australia since she was a young teenager. 'If only you could come with us to Australia, Larry.'

I was taken by surprise and I knew she was being sincere. While my heart ached and I longed for her, I was too scared of going to such a hot climate.

I looked away as I said no. My stubborn, foolish heart ached for her love.

'What about New Zealand, then?' she suggested. 'I think you would like it, it's got a nice climate. I'd say Auckland would suit you better. It's a very green and picturesque country. Larry, are you listening to me at all? I did love you.'

I gazed at the fast-flowing waters. She was in my arms, our lips found each other. To me it was like being in a beautiful dream. 'If only you could stay here, I'm sure we could find a way. I'd make you happy here in Yorkshire.'

She raised up to face me. Her voice was sincere. 'If I were to stay in England, it would have to be in Yorkshire. Like I said, it's Yorkshire for me. But I'd like you to know I would stay with you, Larry. But you are welcome to come with us to Australia and I do understand your reason why you can't. I did love you.' Her eyes met mine.

I took out the poem I wrote for her, 'It's Yorkshire For Me', and gave it to her. As she read it, I gazed at the waters below.

So Pale is the moonlight by the river I see
Through a window on high from your home in Bingley
As I gaze o'er the green with a clear crystal view
I remember the good times – the sad were so few.
The Moors, Shipley Glen and lovely Bingley
I remember you saying 'It's Yorkshire for me.'

The moon tonight will shine bright and clear
On the calm crystal waters that flow through Yorkshire
By bracken and thorn and many a small town
Through the window of my dreams I have watched you
   flow down,
The Moors, Shipley Glen and lovely Bingley
I remember you saying 'It's Yorkshire for me.'

As I closed my eyes beneath the old oak tree
Where the Ayre quietly flows through lovely Bingley
By the evergreen banks that I know so well
Sure I can faintly hear the Village Church bell.
The Moors, Shipley Glen and lovely Bingley
I remember you saying 'It's Yorkshire for me.'

Your sweet voice I can hear, calling to me
As I dream of the river that flows through Bingley
I see the ripple on the waters, ever gentle and clear
How I long to be with you by the lovely River Ayre
The Moors, Shipley Glen and lovely Bingley
I remember you saying 'It's Yorkshire for me.'

For a long moment there was little I could think of doing, except to stare at the calm waters. I wanted to hear what her opinion of it was. Suddenly I glanced at her. Her smile looked sweeter than ever. 'Oh, Larry, you are such a romantic,' she said. She smiled, wiped her eyes and, in a swift, loving movement, her arms were embracing me.

'I know you've fallen in love with me,' she said softly and drew a breath. Then she added, 'You promised me you wouldn't.'

'I am very weak when it comes to matters of the heart. More so when someone as beautiful as you is involved.'

All she did was laugh at me. I said, 'Well, you know how I feel about you.' As she drew closer, I desired her so much my actions got the better of me. She laughed, 'No, no, Larry, not out here. Tonight in my place it will be much more comfortable.'

Our farewell gift to each other, I thought with a smile.

16

Helen convinced me that New Zealand would be the best place for me to make a life, and I decided to stay in Bradford while I saved up for my ticket. I settled into my new lodgings with an Irish family in Bradford and I became friends of the man of the house. Frank was a soft-spoken Dublin man who worked as an accounts clerk with the High Class confectioners/bakers in Bradford. He showed me around the place, and then set me up with a job.

I took it. It would pay for my trip to New Zealand. However, I was taken on with an immediate start on the 11pm night shift. I didn't have much strength after my long illness in Jersey. But Frank's wife, Nora, along with her mum, Mary Rose, promised to build me up in preparation for my forthcoming voyage to New Zealand. Frank took me on long walks to Shipley Glen, over bracken and thorn and along by old deserted woollen mills that housed the ghosts of the industrial past. I began to feel strong again. At weekends I'd ramble off alone with my dreams of Helen, the English teacher. As I stood on a small wooden bridge across the Aire, I gazed fondly across to the Bingley cricket ground. The sun was casting long shadows as it lowered to kiss the plush velvet lawn. A golden October day.

I was to set off in late November for my trip of a lifetime on board the P&O cruise liner *Orchades*. The ticket was £170, which was really expensive in those days. But I had money saved from working in Jersey until I took ill and I was earning at least £16 a week on the night shift in Bradford. I'll be okay for sure, I thought.

In mid-October the weather grew much colder. I'd been out walking with Frank. When we arrived home Nora handed me an envelope. I pulled it open. The warm, fragrant scent sent shivers up through my body. It read: 'Hi, Larry. Will miss you. Bon voyage. Love Helen and Gloria.'

I just felt ill. I was shaken. I heard Mary call out to me. 'What is it? You don't look well, does he, Nora?'

'Come over and sit yerself by the fire, young man. 'Tis like you'd seen a ghost.' Mary pulled up an armchair and I fell into it.

'Now tell me who sent the card to yeh. Was she an old flame from some place you've been to and left her behind?'

I held out the card and stared into the open log fire. Mary's voice broke the silence.

'I knew it. I was right, mind yeh. I could tell you carried scars and be japers, I'd swear yours run deep.'

I muttered, 'You are dead right, ma'am.'

'Larry,' offered Frank. 'Don't take too much heed in what old Mary has to say. She thinks you are on yer way out. She will have you dead and gone before Christmas. Isn't that right, Mary?'

'Dinner is ready, folks, and enough of that pessimism now and leave the lad alone. He's homesick. Can't you see he's sick? Lovesick and homesick,' added Mary. ''Tis time yeh found a good woman that will make a home for yeh. Cook good food and be there for yeh when you need her. Now eat up that plate of beef stew, son. 'Twill do you good, now, and 'twill build you up.'

'It will do yeh no harm anyway,' said Nora.

The next morning Mary served breakfast to me. Scrambled eggs and bacon and beans. I felt very tired and somewhat nauseous. I went up the steep stairs. My room was on the third floor beside the bathroom. Last thing I recall of that almost fateful morning was the smell of bacon and eggs. As I stepped into the bathroom on the top floor I collapsed. It was much later when I opened my eyes. To my horror and shock I could see white coats, bright lights, nurses taking my pulse. I cried. Then I heard a deep, soft Scottish voice.

'Oh gosh, no, no. Not again,' I cried out. I was in shock and in awful pain.

'Do yeh know where you are, young man?' I nodded and muttered, 'No, no.' I felt scared. I remember vividly the moment. How could I ever forget his words. 'I'm a doctor and you have been in here with us. This is the Bradford Royal Infirmary. You are very, very lucky you are still with us. We in fact thought we had lost you. But the bad news is you have suffered a great deal due to a perforated duodenal ulcer. But we got you in good time. You are going to be with us for quite some time. Until the New Year.'

I reached out and pulled at his arm or hand. I simply cried out, 'No, no, no. I can't. I'm booked on a ship to New Zealand in late November. I got to go on it, doctor. It's paid for.'

His tone was much softer. 'I promise you we will take care of everything to get you well again. That includes your voyage to New Zealand. Our people will have that taken care of. So you will have no worries while you are with us. Right now you need to rest.'

I closed my eyes to the bright lights once again. I found grief and heartache without warning. Thoughts of being here as the P&O cruise ship *Orchades* set sail for the twelve thousand-mile voyage made me so sick that I messed up the pure white starched sheets.

Get-well cards arrived. There was one from Helen. I didn't know how she could have found out. As I was left alone I cried for all I had lost.

But then something happened that I hadn't expected: Helen came to visit. She embraced me and I just cried as we held on to each other for a long, precious moment. Her smile was radiant. I felt I'd been raised up by her presence.

'You know, Larry, you are one hell of a survivor. How many lives have you got, Larry? I'm so glad to see you smile through all of this, after all you've been through. How long are they going to keep you in here?'

I drew in a long, deep breath. Gosh, how I tried to control my hurt, my anger, my emotion. 'Till after Christmas,' I said.

Her eyes met mine at that moment, moist and blue. She leaned in over me, her voice a whisper. 'I'm so sorry, Larry. You'll miss your voyage to New Zealand next week. Has everything been taken care of?'

I nodded yes. 'The travel agent returned the full fare I had paid, along with a get-well card. Imagine that, Helen.' I felt her hand squeeze mine. Her presence brought back memories of our time together in her home in Bingley and in her apartment in Jersey. How I dread November, and I always will, I thought then.

She stood up and wished me well. My English teacher left me that Sunday in November with all of her charm, kind thoughts and fond loving memories, knowing I would never see her again. I lay down and closed my eyes as she wished me goodbye.

I left Bradford Royal in the New Year of 1968, fit and fully recovered from my closest call yet. But I've learned old sayings, of which many ring true. Time waits for no one, for rich or poor. I returned to the place I could best call home: Dublin.

Mrs Mooney's words haunted me as I travelled back to Dublin: 'A rolling stone gathers no moss, Pat.' I seemed to have no control over making so many awful heartbreaking decisions. 'You are your own worst enemy, Pat,' May's words rang so true. I cried my heart out on the trip home from Bradford, realising I had no home to actually return home to.

In fact, my past returned to haunt me once I settled back into my usual work in the bakery trade. Though I could never have foreseen it, or planned it, as the blasted shadow of Artane returned to me once more.

17

Once back in my home town, I found a very comfortable self-contained bedsit. The flat was on the third floor of a four-storey Georgian house. Mrs Fiona Ryan, a warm-hearted Tipperary woman, was my new landlady. She quite often invited me to say the Rosary with her in her living room. I quite often agreed to this as she served a nice supper afterwards. Her husband was a civil servant, a very tall, straight and erect man, an ardent Catholic, and far too fond of the drink.

One evening I dropped in to see them. It was about ten o'clock – their prayer time. I noticed he was not there, and then I was ushered out by the Mrs Ryan. She looked very bothered. Suddenly I heard shouting as I walked up the stairs. 'It's him!' I stayed a moment to listen. 'You were with him again, Fiona. I don't trust that new lodger of yours at all now. He's been seeing you. Tell me or I'll go up and drag him down here.' I heard his wife shout at him. 'You're drunk, you fool, as usual. You're not half the man he is. I swear to God on it, and he so young. Look at you, a bloody civil servant – a drunken lout, bedad!' I hurried up to my flat and bolted the door.

Suddenly there was a knock, then a whispering. 'Are you in, Pat? Pat!' I opened the door. She spoke hurriedly. This could only happen to me, I thought. 'You must lock your door and put whatever furniture you can against it – quickly. Have you got any girls with you?' I laughed at the question. 'No. What a pity. None at all. No one loves me, Fiona, any more.' She blushed and began to warn me of her husband. 'He's dangerous. We have a problem. He's an alcoholic and he's drunk and angry. He thinks you and I are seeing each other. You must leave here in the morning. I have a safe house for you to go to in Castle Avenue. Don't worry, Pat.'

How could he think such a thing? I heard him shout up at her, 'I'll kill him! I'm coming up!' I closed the door and put all the furniture against it. I heard her shout, 'I'm calling the guards. They'll fix you, you mad drunken fool.' I prayed they would hurry.

As I sat waiting to see what was going to happen, a hatchet came through the door. He roared in at me, 'I'll get to you, lover boy. Say the Rosary with my wife, do yeh? I'll say a decade over your dead body for yeh! Let me in!'

I felt petrified as he smashed the door of the flat, and I had to hold him off. It was a fight for my life as I could see the hatchet in his hand. He was over six feet tall. He pushed me, then swung the hatchet down at me. I sidestepped, and as I grabbed hold of him, the guards arrived. He held me by the throat and I was really struggling at that point. His wife was shouting to me, 'Hit him! Kill him! Kill him!' The guards then led him away. I followed them downstairs and watched as he faced his wife in the hall. He swore at her. 'I was right, Fiona, all the while. I knew he wasn't coming in to say the Rosary with you. Oh, no, Fiona, you were seeing him also. Your own pretty toyboy.'

I found new lodgings at two that morning, in a bedsitter in Castle Avenue. I felt I had been involved in a nightmare.

When I took a walk later to get to know the area, I came across a bakery and confectionery shop. I looked up at the name: W. Ferguson and Sons. I thought I'd try my luck for a job. Ten minutes later I walked out smiling. I was to start at eight the next morning. The money was fine: sixteen pounds ten a week, including a fully cooked breakfast, dinner and tea every day. I was over the moon.

Ferguson's was a lovely place to work in. I loved getting up in the mornings to go to work, and I learnt quite a bit about confectionery and cake mixing there. I will never leave here, I thought. I can finally settle down.

A strange thing happened a few weeks later. The boss took a call from Artane School, from the Brother in charge of settling boys when they were sixteen. Mr Ferguson called me into his little office, which was beneath the stairs leading to the famous Ferguson's Tea Rooms. He sat me down and began to explain that my old school had requested that we take a boy, if not two, and train them, as the school was to close down as an industrial boarding school by the summer. I took a deep breath. For a moment there was silence. I was about to leave when he added, 'By the way, I may need you to come with me.' As I hurried home that evening I felt the shadow of my past engulf me. Why me? I thought.

Mr Ferguson called me in again a few days later. 'I'm going to ask you to go up to Artane with me. I've decided to take a boy off their hands and give him training. If he works out, then I may take a second. We need you, Patrick, to help us out and to help us choose the right one. I hear Brother O'Connor has quite a few orphan boys on his hands who have to be fixed up, as they hope to close by June.'

It was 1969, over ten years since I had left. The trip brought back memories I had tried to suppress. As the car turned up the Malahide Road, within minutes I could see Marino Christian Brothers' School, and then the dark, dreary buildings of Artane School, which dominated the whole area of Donnycarney and Artane, as they do to this day. Instantly I felt emotionally distressed.

As the car turned to go up the main avenue, my heart beat faster and my hands were sweaty. We drove slowly up the avenue. Ferguson looked surprised at the neatness of the grounds and at how big the place was.

I noticed Brother Joe O'Connor coming down the steps of the office. I could see he was delighted we came. He remembered me well as I introduced him to my boss. It was at that point I got the feeling I had never left – yet here I was, about to choose an orphan lad to come and learn a trade with us.

I stood inside the infirmary, which had been turned into a small dormitory, and I was really taken aback: the rows of beds so neatly made up; the centre aisle polished to a glittering shine; the statue of Our Lady and the holy water font.

I could clearly remember it all. I was sure I could hear the cries of the boys being flogged. It all came back to me. In many ways it was a blessing, being asked to go there, as my past had to come out into the open, and it reminded me of what my childhood really had been.

I stared silently at the boys. Their hair was crew-cut and they were neatly dressed in their Artane serge cloth and hobnailed boots, and that awful lonesome, hungry appearance brought it all back to me. Ten years had passed, although it seemed like only a few months.

I helped choose the boy. The choice was not a difficult one, as there were only three who wanted to work in a bakery. I saw this small, tubby, fresh-faced lad with a sad look on his round face. He gave me a slight grin. I could see he was longing for a break and hoped I would choose him. Brother O'Connor gave me a rather dry smile, as though he suspected I was thinking of the time he battered my bottom so badly I thought my buttocks were two lumps of rare meat, and, what's more, I knew he enjoyed every second of it. He was just as cruel and perverted as the Macker, the Bucko and Hellfire, and so many more who got pleasure out of abusing the kids in their care.

When I got home to my flat in Castle Avenue I was drained in so many ways. I lay down and closed my eyes. All I could think of was my past.

About this time I saw an advertisement for a car going very cheaply. I called to the flat in Leinster Road, Rathmines, to see it. Who should answer the doorbell but the bold Quickfart himself. We chatted for what seemed like hours in his bedsitter. I gave him all the news I had – including what happened to me in London. When he heard he hit the roof with laughter. 'Did you ever meet Oxo on your travels, Paddy?' he asked me. 'As a matter of fact I did. He worked in Lyon's in London,' I told him.

I could see the tears in his eyes. He just talked and talked, about Artane in general and about Oxo. Some of the memories were painful for him. Suddenly I glanced at my watch and shouted, 'Bloody hell, I've got to be going. Will you show me the car? Maybe you'll let me have it very reasonable?' I smiled at him. I was hoping to get his mind off his past. 'Come on, Quickie, I'd like to test-drive that car.' I was relieved to see him smile.

He stood, shrugged his broad shoulders and agreed. I bought the car from him for about £160. 'You know where to find me, Paddy, if it breaks down.' I enjoyed a good laugh at that one, as he moved about more than even I did.

18

In Autumn 1970, I was quite honestly gutted to hear that Ferguson's were closing down. In late November, actually. So I had no choice. I was glad I had my passage booked to New Zealand. Mr Ferguson told me I was doing the right thing in emigrating. I believed strongly that I was, and decided that even if I got homesick I would stay at least twelve months and see a bit of the world before returning.

The *Shota Rustaveli* was a Russian liner, and I was one of two thousand people from Ireland, England, Malta and Cyprus on board. It was enormous and spotlessly clean, and when I walked up the gangway into the shining corridors I felt as if I was in a hospital! For the five weeks I was on board, the great liner was like an incredible floating city.

My first walk around after I had settled into my cabin, which was a four-berth, became a walk into another romance – within hours of coming on board! I was watching the English coastline fade slowly into the distance when I noticed a slim, tall young woman coming towards me. She had dark shoulder-length hair and was holding a cigarette. She looked at me and smiled. I got a whiff of her perfume and was attracted to her casual, film-star charm and her tantalising smile. Just like the beautiful French au pair, Maria.

She spoke softly. 'Have you got a match for me?'

'I'm so sorry, I don't smoke, I said apologetically. She put away the cigarette. I was overwhelmed by her beauty.

'My name is Andrea. I'm from New Zealand.' Her hand was outstretched and mine reached slowly to hold it as I introduced myself. What fine long fingers, I thought. I held on to her hand, as she wasn't letting go. I felt at ease. We were alone on deck, and we both stood staring at the distant coastline. I imagined I was dreaming.

Andrea turned and began to move along the deck. I followed with a certain reluctance, not sure of myself. Then she paused, long enough for me to catch up. I began to feel this could be my lucky day – and all this in the first few hours. It did strike me as something of a fantasy.

We were now in a short darkened passageway, and the only sound was from the seagulls. My hand seemed to rest lightly at first around her waist. Her lips closed upon mine. Her long fingers rested in my hair. Losing any clear notions I had in respect of her charm and elegance, I let myself go as scenes of the flesh took hold of me.

A light came on that brightened up the passageway. I noticed a huge deckhand, then another. They passed some comment and then roared with laughter. 'Come on, Andrea, I'll see you back to your cabin.'

Before she went I could at last see how she really looked in the bright light. I was overwhelmed by her attractiveness. She asked me if she could share my table in the dining room. We had a table for two for the entire voyage.

The trip to New Zealand was more of an adventure than a sea voyage. Life aboard the ship was fantastic. I took part in stage shows, the best of them *South Pacific*. They organised a poetry reading, with pride of place for anyone who recited their own poetry. I was driven to write at that time, so I entered for the reading, which was to be held in the great dining room after the evening dinner, as a form of cabaret.

On the night of the poetry reading Andrea came to dinner with me. She wanted to hear my poems. She looked beautiful in her red dress with a blue silk sash around her waist. Her smile simply radiated confidence and encouragement for me as my name was called out. I was being either honoured or disposed of quickly – I wasn't sure which – but I was the first to perform. I had to stand on stage before two thousand people, the captain, the officers and crew and hear the host describe me as a new Irish poet. I took out my first poem, called 'Some Mother's Son'. It's about a young man washed up on the sands at the end of the

Second World War, whom I learnt of while on my first visit to the Isle of Man in 1959. I followed that by reading 'The Coal Fire', for which I received a rapturous applause.

I tried to leave the stage, but everybody stood up and began chanting for more, and I was led back. I tried to get a glimpse of Andrea, and when I spotted her I felt fine. I wanted her to hear the poem I wrote with her in mind and dedicated to her, 'The MS *Shota Rustaveli*'.

From the moment I got up at around nine every morning until I went to my cabin for the night between midnight and two, there was always something for me to do. Each morning I took charge of the keep-fit fanatics' class at half ten. There was a writers' workshop at noon. One-act plays were performed at night in the main lounge in front of over 500 people, and I took part in these too.

After lunch there were sports, from basketball to clay pigeon shooting. There were three small cinemas, which showed the very best films. There was also a choice of bars, lounges, dancing, cabaret, and stage shows. I was eager to participate in all the sports and shows, and in this way I was always kept active. Andrea was always close at hand but she was a real mystery to me. I couldn't figure her out at all.

When we arrived in Auckland, the sun was extremely hot. I was dressed in a pure wool three-piece suit, and I was stared at as I walked down the gangway. God, I muttered, how am I going to stick this heat? Andrea came towards me, and once again I blew it – as always! I felt she had ignored me at times to be with other men friends at night in clubs and at the roulette tables. I thought she was simply using me to suit herself. When Andrea asked me if I had a place to stay, I felt cold and distant towards her.

I looked at her, and without really giving it a second thought I said, 'I'll stay in Auckland. After all, I've come twelve thousand miles to be here. I'll find some place to stay.' She looked sad as she silently went on her way. Little did I realise that I would never again see the beautiful New Zealand girl who had stolen my heart in the first hours of the long voyage. Once again I blew it, perhaps. She was sincere, but I couldn't take the chance after what happened with Noreen.

Afterwards I felt lost, lonesome and foolish as I settled in to my room in the YMCA hostel in the city. I must admit that down through the years I have made some dreadful decisions that later left me sick with self-pity.

There were times when I wanted to end it all, and once I actually tried. I was out along the beach at Bream Bay, and I was feeling so homesick that I would have offered everything I owned for the sound of an Irish voice; and a piece of Irish music on the radio had me in tears. I walked into the water from the golden stretch of sand. I simply wanted to keep on walking, when I took a fall over some rocks beneath the water. I heard a voice shouting, 'You okay out there, mate?' Within moments I was lifted out to safety, with blood oozing from a head wound. I opened my eyes to find a young woman cleaning my wounds while her boyfriend helped her. I was taken by surprise when I realised she was topless!

His accent was a mixture of Yorkshire and New Zealand. 'Sorry, mate, for the way we're dressed, or undressed.' He smiled. 'We come here at weekends and swim out to the reef like this – quite a lot of us do in these parts.' He looked at his girlfriend and said, 'This is Jean. She comes from a place near Te Aroha, near Morrinsville.' He shook my hand. 'I'm Erin.'

Odd name, I thought, and smiled. Blood was getting into my eyes and I felt dizzy. I just heard him say, 'I've got an Irish passport,' and then I passed out.

I had a good nurse looking after me in Jean. I was brought back to their house near Wellsford, where I stayed for a few days. Jean was a teacher with first-aid experience. She was the kind of girl I dreamed of ending up with.

After I had settled down in the YMCA in Auckland, I began to find my way around the city. I searched for a new start. However, I could find none; no job offers came my way.

I had no choice. I realised I had to find work in a bakery, or face life on the dole. No way, I thought, was I going to join the dole queue in New Zealand having come across the Equator 12,000 miles. While out walking I happened to come across a home bakery on a busy main road. A sale sign was in the window. I entered and a tall gentleman came to meet me. 'How can I help you, mate?' He's English, I thought. For a while I worked with him and his wife. Eventually I agreed to take over the leasehold and I opened the Home Bakery as Laurence's Home Bakery, as Laurence is my middle name. I held a small opening party.

I was unaware of some of New Zealand's customs, and I ran into a few sticky problems. I put on what I thought was a fine spread of food and drink, but as the guests arrived I noticed there was going to be a far bigger crowd than I invited. How was I going to have enough for everyone? Some of the guests I already knew from the voyage. I had kept their addresses and I was glad to meet them again.

I had met Dave on board ship, and we kept in touch. He was a mature young school teacher, born in New Zealand to English parents. He quickly became my adviser as I tumbled from one problem to the next. He pointed out that when one invites a Maori to a party, they believe they can bring the clan. It doesn't always happen, but in my case I had invited an English lad who was married to a Maori chief's daughter, and she turned up with over fifteen members of their family.

I began to wonder why they had all brought their own

food. I asked Dave, and he told me that it's the custom in New Zealand to bring your own 'tucka' and drink to such gatherings. So, after my initial worries, I was left with a hell of a lot of uneaten food.

Just before Christmas the priest, Father John Davaro, was outside the church to greet everyone personally after Mass. When he came to me his first words were, 'So you're the new man in our parish – just in from the old sod. So tell me, where are you for dinner, Patrick?'

I told him, 'I'm alone, Father. I've just moved into the bakery in Ponsonby. It's called Laurence's Home Bakery – formerly Don's Cake Tin.'

'Yes, yes, I know it. Too bad – it's not nice to be left alone at Christmastime for dinner. So you'll come with me to my mother's up in Helensville for a few days? Mother will take care of you. She's a wonderful old lady, Patrick, and she'll simply spoil you, I can tell you now, just to get all the news from home, you see.'

I readily agreed, thrilled that I had someone to talk to during the days ahead. I believed that by keeping up my faith and praying at intervals during the day, good things would really happen and it would help me to settle into my new home. On the way up to Helensville I noticed that the beaches were crowded. I smiled as I thought of Ireland. To tell the truth, I was missing the foggy dew and the frosty winter mornings.

Also, I was having a tough time of it making a living. I soon realised I had made another awful decision. The bakery trade was slow: New Zealanders on the whole didn't go in much for cakes, or indeed sweet things. Once more I was left cursing my rotten decisions.

I began to make Irish soda bread. The brown soda wouldn't sell, but the Maori really went for my white bread. However, they soon got fed up buying it. They invited me to the home of a chief, and I was obliged to show them how I made the bread. Soon after that business fell away.

Winter started to draw nearer. Suddenly I began to enjoy going to bed at night, as the climate was much like home now. I joined the GAA club for the forthcoming football and hurling league. I was asked by Peter, a new friend, to join the soccer club he was in, and I obliged. I enjoyed every moment playing alongside Peter. Soccer was at about the same level as any one of the junior leagues at home, but no better. Rugby was the main New Zealand sport. There were only about five or six Gaelic clubs in Auckland, and Celtic were the best of a poor lot.

The winter was wet but mild. I decided to try to sell the lease on the bakery, but there were bakeries for sale in every second street. The country was troubled by England joining the EEC, and concerned about their beef, butter, lamb and cheese trade.

I was struck by the many good things in New Zealand, and I realised it far more after I had returned to Ireland for the New Year. Going into Auckland for a bit of shopping was made more comfortable by the practice of having a white line dividing the city footpaths in two. To walk up the main footpaths you had to stay inside on the left-hand or shop-window side; people walking down had to remain on the outside of the pavement. It was all very orderly. You could only cross the street with the wardens, who were at special pedestrian crossings; anyone caught crossing through the traffic got an automatic on-the-spot fine. Churchgoers always went into the church rather than standing at the back. On the whole, people were most orderly, and more tolerant than I had expected.

I noticed as time passed that Irish people stuck closely together and rarely mixed with other nationals, yet I found that I was odd in that sense: I liked to mix with New Zealanders and people from foreign lands.

19

One afternoon in the spring of 1971 I was cleaning up in the shop. Business had not been good; I suited myself when it was time to close. Just as I was about to finish for the day, a tall, middle-aged man entered the shop. I had the cakes and bread that were left over ready to bring down to the convent. This, I found, was the best way of parting with the leftovers. I had been advised by business friends in the area that it was very bad for business to give your goods away for free, even stale bread. They had a point, but as far as I was concerned, it wouldn't make me any poorer.

'Hello, Father. What can I do for you?'

He came closer. 'I'm a missionary Brother, not a priest.' He smiled. 'I travel Asia in my work for the missions. Most of our members have to do some work on the land every day and teach others the same.'

He looked familiar. From where I was standing he looked like Brother Simon Davaro, the man I had shared a room with, the man from Artane. But could it be him? If it was, he had certainly changed; he was no longer the slim, handsome young man he once had been.

'Would you like some tea, Brother?' I plugged in the kettle. As we sat down for tea, I noticed his movements. I was almost certain it was Brother Simon. I decided to test him. 'You must travel a fair bit, sir.'

'Yes, Patrick, I travel a great deal in my line of work – and I need young, bright, unattached workers like you to join the missions. You'll be well rewarded.'

How did he know my name was Patrick? A stranger would think I was named Laurence, because of the sign over the door. I watched as he lit a cigarette. I had to ask him. 'Were you ever in Artane School on your travels?'

There was silence now. I kept my eyes on him. When he spoke again he had lost much of his self-confidence and dominant air. 'Yes, I was a Christian Brother. I also spent a short term in a place called Letterfrack.'

It was he. I knocked a cup over on the floor, and moved quickly to clean it up.

Changing the subject smartly, he went into great detail about his present work. I reached to the press on the wall and drew out a bottle of Australian red wine that I kept for visitors. I poured him a full glass as he carefully lit another cigarette. 'Many thanks,' he said, as he raised the glass to his lips.

I was interested to know how he became a Christian Brother. Tentatively I asked, 'Was it your own choice that you became a Brother?'

He appeared surprised by my question, and uneasy at first. 'I came from a large family, Pat, being the third-youngest of five brothers and four sisters. My two eldest brothers are priests. One of them, John, is here in Auckland. He's the local priest.'

So that's why he's here, I thought.

He continued, 'My two eldest sisters are nuns. We were promised to the church at an early age. Like a lot of the Brothers, I was sent to a Christian Brothers' boarding school until I was sixteen.' He smiled as he said, 'I had a choice, Patrick.' He paused for a moment and sipped the wine. 'Yes, two choices: the priesthood or the brotherhood.' I laughed heartily. He drew on the cigarette and said, 'My father, who was a tough, no-nonsense County Mayo small farmer, wanted me to go to the Christian Brothers, while my mother, who was gentler and more kind, wished me to join my two elder brothers in the priesthood.'

I waited for him to light another cigarette, then reach for the wine. 'Sure it wasn't a choice at all, damn it. The parish priest was for ever coming through our front door. Many's the time he'd look at me and say, "You'll be joining us soon, Simon, I believe, as soon as you're sixteen." You know, it was a stark choice between romancing a stone and milking a pig. I didn't want either of them, and life as a Christian Brother in the 1940s and '50s was for a lot of us pure hell.

'You see, Pat, in rural Ireland in those days, parents were strongly urged to have big families. It wasn't unusual for the local priest to order a woman in the confessional to have more children as penance for her sins. My own mother told me that. The church was forceful in its teachings in those days, I tell you. My two brothers often joked about hearing Mother's confession. I remember one Christmas the family were all around the table for dinner, when my eldest brother, Seamus, jokingly said, "I'll hear your confession now, Ma, since you missed out for Christmas." As quick as a flash my sister Eileen responded to him: "Now, Father Seamus, Mother has enough poor mouths to feed, thanks to your Catholic Church. Don't you think nine children in one family is enough, or would you prefer that Mother goes on giving birth for her penance until she could field a football team?" You see, in those days, son, there was no real choice at all.'

'Was it hard for you and your fellow Brothers in Artane?'

'At times, yes; but it wasn't just because it was Artane or its harsh military system. Oh, no – on the contrary, the food was the best I'd ever tasted. We were at all times given the best when it came to food; but it was at night I found the difference: the loneliness of the place and how I feared being attacked in a dark corridor. I feared being a failure, and I also had to toe the line. In some ways I knew the life was not for me.

'The system grew on me. I couldn't fail my superiors. I could never have let them down. I also feared the harsh life of a Christian Brother; not being able to marry or get to know girls. I did have sexual feelings, you know.

'From Artane I was despatched off to Letterfrack. If you think Artane was tough, well, then, Letterfrack was hell, me lad. It was my job from the first day to take out those boys who were listed to be punished. Myself and a chap called Damian were on duty for unruly boys. We got them out at six each morning, and their punishment was that they cut and draw turf across the bog for long hours. Any boy who didn't conform had to be flogged. We used buckets of salted cold water to throw over them afterwards. I still lie awake at nights at the sight of the blood from their thighs and buttocks, running down on to the cold stone floor. I got to like flogging the tough boys while they were strapped up. It began to eat into me, and I began to feel like a jailer; but the sexual abuse I couldn't tolerate at all, at all.

'Letterfrack, Patrick, was like deportation and isolation. It really began to affect me. I was flogging boys' naked bottoms in my sleep. I began to have nightmares. It all changed so suddenly. Perhaps it was for the best, really.'

We stood outside my small bakery shop. It was very hot. We began to walk. 'What became of your friend Damian?' We headed towards the harbour. 'Damian got married soon after he left the order, just as I did. Poor Damian, that dreaded disease TB got him. He had a beautiful wife. I only met her once, and that was at his wedding in Dublin.'

The view of Auckland Bay was breathtaking. I turned to Simon and said, 'It's like one of the wonders of the world watching the great ships on the horizon as they come and go across the world, bringing people to a new country to start again.'

He smiled warmly and with a loud voice he said, 'Well, me lad, I couldn't have put it better meself. You certainly would make a good preacher. You have a way with words.'

He went on, 'So tell me, Patrick, have you any intention of getting married, making a home for yourself?'

Caught unawares, I said, 'Yes, I'd like that if I found someone nice who would accept me and my ways, Brother.'

As he exhaled, I studied the big man. 'In many ways,' he said, 'you are like me, Pat. A sheltered life would suit you, I'm certain of it.'

I looked away towards the Bay. But you got married: what happened to Laura? I will always remember her picture on the dressing table in Molly's.

'Laura? Yes, poor girl.' He sighed. 'It was doomed from the

start, I believe. I stayed too long in the order, and my health suffered, you see. I was having constant nightmares and awful dreams of my past. All the floggings. I loved Laura but she couldn't live with me – my strict ways, among other things. The last I heard she was living in Boston.

'I was ill prepared for married life, Molly was right. She really did shame me when she told me of my nightmares and disturbing the lodgers. It was so close to the wedding I couldn't turn back, you understand.'

I noticed his hand shake as he lit another cigarette. It was at that moment I felt sorry for this man who once abused me only to feel sorry for me later. I liked him because he was more human than the rest of them. He drew hard on the cigarette, then glanced at me.

'It was an experience I regret deeply, marrying Laura. Her parents blamed me on her losing the baby, and her awful depression that followed. You see, it was a dreadful time. I was not fit to be married, more suited to a sheltered life, I'd say.'

'So you wouldn't recommend a married life for me then?'

His gaze rested on me, and his tone was deep and sincere. 'Perhaps you are different after all. You never abused boys or had to beat them as I had to. It's not easy to bury the past, not a bleak past such as mine.'

'Are you contented now?'

His smile returned, 'Indeed I am. A sheltered life suits me.'

Suddenly he started a dreadful bout of coughing. ''Tis the lungs, me boy. Will you join us, Pat?'

Thoughts of the girls I had known flooded my mind. 'What would I do, Brother? Would I travel a lot?' I smiled at the idea of it.

'Good Lord, no, Pat. Very few of us enjoy that. 'Tis my job to find new recruits.'

'Then where would I be based, and what exactly would my job be?' I liked the idea of teaching, as I was certain that was what he meant when he said I'd make a fine preacher.

'Well, you need a direct answer, I see. You don't beat about the bush. Well, Patrick, I believe you would make a fine shepherd on our large sheep farm, and you could also use your skill as a baker for a few months to begin with, to help clear your mind, and you would attend lectures at night.'

By the time he finished, my mind was on the soft rain of Ireland. The feeling for home and my passion for love were too great. I realised then that New Zealand wasn't for me and that I desperately needed to go back home. I smiled at him. How could I tell him I didn't want to mind his sheep? I said, 'It was lovely meeting you again, Brother, but my heart is in Ireland.'

For a long, silent moment we both gazed out across Auckland Bay. My eyes rested on the blue horizon as a tall ship appeared.

It was such an odd experience meeting Brother Simon again. He was so much older and heavier than the man who came to share a room with me, and so different to the Brother I had known at school.

I walked away, knowing I'd never see him again; yet he was a far happier man than I was, and that bothered me for a long time, even as I sold up the business and travelled down to Wellington for my voyage home. It was with great sadness that I learned of his death a few years later.

20

On 18 November I stepped on board the great Italian liner *Angelina Lauro*, with over two thousand other passengers bound for Europe, on a voyage that would take me to Chile, Uruguay, Argentina, Brazil, Portugal, Spain, England, and home to Dublin. There was a terrific feeling on board, and I knew I was going to enjoy it. I chose the *Angelina Lauro* because of its fantastic route.

The first port of call after the Magellan Strait and Tierra del Fuego was Punta Arenas in Chile. It was freezing cold, and the streets were full of deep cracks. I never got to meet any of the ordinary people, but a tour was organised for a party of us to meet a few generals, and I was asked to give them recipes for soda bread and Irish stew.

I was looking forward to Rio de Janeiro. The weather was getting so hot and I had heard so much about the famous Copacabana golden mile that I was ready to plunge into the sea once I set foot on the beach.

I met a few English and Welsh lads, and they had planned to hire a minibus in Rio to see the sights; they invited me to join them. The driver stopped every few miles and asked for more money, and the lads simply emptied their pockets and wallets to coax him to drive on. It was a crazy trip. I was broke from paying the driver at the start, and I felt sorry for the lads who had brought more cash with them to buy presents.

The driver was going to dump us all out when we were about ten miles from Rio. As one of the Welsh lads reckoned, we had paid enough to buy the minibus as it was. When the driver threatened to leave us unless we paid him again, one of the lads lost his temper and punched and kicked the driver to the ground. He shouted at us and threatened to go to the police. The lads gave him a choice: 'Drive us as you were paid to do, or we take over the bus.'

He refused. I took the wheel and shouted, 'Let's hit the road, lads!' and drove back to Rio without further problems.

We stopped in Copacabana for a swim, and couldn't wait to strip off. The heat was overpowering as I ran out on to the beach. I turned and shouted to the others that it was a high tide. I noticed a very tall lifeguard some yards away. He shouted something, but I couldn't understand him, and didn't know if he was shouting at me or at the girls who just passed me, both of whom were topless.

The beach seemed to dip sharply into the sea. I noticed the

English lads standing on the wall. One of them shouted, 'You going in, Paddy, or are yeh scared, mate?' Without any further encouragement I was in, and suddenly I lost my footing, as I could feel no sand beneath me. I began to shout frantically for help, but a wave went over me, and I was certain I was done for. Then a mighty dark wave swept over me, and I was pushed towards the stony beach, trying desperately to cling on to the stones. The arms of the lifeguard began clutching at me. I tried to stand up but it was too steep. The lifeguard was only a few feet in front of me as the next wave surged upon us, knocking us both forward. He grabbed hold of my wrist and held on, and pulled me to safety, with the aid of the English lads, who were pulling him.

I stood close to the lifeguard, thanking him. He spoke in Portuguese, and then he shouted at the English lads, who were enjoying a laugh at my expense: 'You English all mad, just like your English friend here.' I laughed.

As I lay in my cabin later that night, my thoughts were not on the drama in the high tide at Copacabana but on the twenty thousand huts on the hillsides overlooking the famous resort city: huts made of tin, wooden boxes and even of cardboard that were homes to the poor people of Rio. I felt ashamed that I couldn't offer any help to any of them, except a smile and my prayers. I have never forgotten the faces of the women and the hungry children I have never forgotten. Whenever I think of

Rio de Janeiro and the splendid richness that is Copacabana I think of them, and their most famous footballer, Pelé.

Our last port of call was Vigo in Spain. On this occasion I decided to go it alone and see the very attractive Spanish port my way, by foot. I followed the road to the centre of the city, then walked along the dusty road as it turned and twisted into the hillside.

I got the smell of bread being baked. I followed the lovely aroma, which brought me along a narrow track up the hillside, where I stopped by a farmhouse high above the sea. There was a fantastic view of the port and of the liner. The sky was deep blue, and I could see for miles. An old man answered my knock, and I asked for a drink of water. I was led into the oldest bakery I'd ever seen, and handed a full glass of red wine. They all spoke a few words of English. The bread was all made by hand. I showed them that I was a baker; I took up the peel and drew crusty, well-baked bread from an oven that was a hole in the wall cut into the mountain.

The wine began to affect me, and as I finished my glass it was quickly filled again. The bakery was part of the farm and vineyard. They made their own wine, a beautiful red fruity wine. When I reappeared outside I was seeing two ships!

I turned to say goodbye and I was offered a further glass, and the bakers came out to the horseshoe-shaped door and stood smiling at me. I wanted to have a chat with them, and I could see they wished the same. We settled for nods and winks, and I drank a further glass of their red wine.

It was so flaming hot outside I began to wonder how I was going to get back down over the rough terrain. I looked at them, then at my watch and towards the ship. They must have understood me: a horse and cart pulled up, and the men cheered loudly as I got in. I could have cried as I waved goodbye to them. 'Salt of the earth,' I said to myself as I left.

I was home in Dublin for Christmas 1971. I quickly found a job in KC Bakery and Confectioners in the north city where I was told I was the manager! When I went and informed the few bakers, they simply roared laughing! Tony explained: 'You see, Paddy, the boss tells every lad he takes on these days the same thing. Soon he'll have a house full of bakery managers!' I got the message.

There was a lot of talk among the lads about joining the union. I kept my mouth shut on this one, as I didn't want to walk into it again. I had a feeling I had made a bad decision in coming back, as I soon realised that some things never changed.

I was standing at the oven with the boss the day the union secretary walked into the KC Bakery. With him was the union president.

The boss spoke softly, like a whisper, as I stood by the oven. 'What's going on, Pat?'

I was amazed he didn't know. I got it off my chest quickly. 'The Bakers' Union are here, sir. Tony and the lads are going to join, and if you don't agree with them, they'll leave, sir.'

'The bloody union my arse! Who needs them!' He stood facing me. 'How many will join, do you know?'

After a deep breath – and I felt sure I was going to be out of a job after his next question – I said, 'All the lads, sir; I'm not sure about the girls.'

He looked flushed. He spoke softly for a big man, and I liked him. 'They can have their union, they're welcome to it wherever it is, but it won't be in here. Never. I built my business without it.'

I could see his concern. He was apprehensive about change, but though I sympathised with him, in my heart I couldn't agree with him. He asked abruptly: 'Are you with them?' He expected me to say no: not even the lads knew that I would jump at the chance to join. I answered briefly. 'Yes, I'm with them. I always wanted to join, since I left school, sir.'

'Okay, then, get your coat and join them, and good luck.'

I went home that evening out of a job, but with the news that I was to report to the Bakers' Union in 46 Gardiner Street, Dublin, at six the following morning.

Peter Flanagan, the secretary of the union, was a real father figure to me. That he had turned me down on the many occasions I had tried to join since I left Artane in 1958 was of no real significance. He quickly pointed out to me and the other lads that we would only be jobbers, but that if we were kept in any one union bakery for two or more years we would then become fully fledged members of the union. I was told then to report to Jack Barrett, the foreman in Boland's bakery in Grand Canal Street.

I felt proud but apprehensive as I set off from what was then known as the Hall in Gardiner Street and stepped it out, Artane style, along the city quays.

My first impression of Boland's was that it resembled a railway station. There were tracks and belts all over the place. As far as I could see, almost everything was moving, overhead and on the ground. Even the huge ovens were travelling. I had never seen such plant before, and I was instantly confused by it all. As I was a skilled tablehand-baker, I began to wonder what all the fuss was about that prevented ex-Artaners like myself from setting foot on their sacred union soil. As far as I could see, a pig farmer could do the work just as well as any of those men who served four-year apprenticeships.

I was surrounded by old acquaintances. 'Oh, God,' I moaned as I was put working alongside my first foreman in Bradley's Home Bakery in Fairview, Eddie Kavanagh. For some reason Eddie was known in Boland's as the Virginian. There were a few other ex-Artaners; and soon I came face to face with my old friend Mando.

It was an experience to be sent for my first tea break and told to report to Jemser's oven, where the lidded pans were baked off. I got my mug of tea and followed the Virginian over to a table. One man said in a loud voice, 'I don't mean to sound rude or harsh to yeh, just fuckin' tell us where yeh served your time.'

Another man shouted, 'Yeah, give us your pedigree, mate. Who'd you serve your time with, shithead?'

I looked at the hardened men around the table, and knew I was seated in the wrong place. These men don't like strange faces, or jobbers perhaps. I looked at the Virginian, and he gave me the wink. I was glad to go back and join the chain gang at Jemser's oven.

The Virginian warned me not to tell them too much, and not to take them too seriously, but I felt confused by it all. 'Who's Jemser?' I asked the Virginian; a tough character passing by shouted back at us, 'Jem Kelly, yeh mutton-headed fucker.'

Jemser's oven was down alongside the wall. I looked at the men: tired, overweight, hardened, their working whites worn and tattered and more grey than white. There were five of them, and I was to make up the gang to six, which was called Kelly's chain gang. As Jemser controlled the speed of the huge oven, I followed the gang as we moved in a circle to pick up a long lid from a bin, grab a shape with the pan inside and force the lid on to it, then place the shape on the slow-moving oven. We had to follow in the circle for over one and a half hours, until the shapes were all on the oven.

By the time they were all up it was time for another break, and the lads were glad to get away for a smoke. Once again I was the odd one out, as I didn't smoke.

I was completely disillusioned by the end of my first week with the total lack of skill or craft required to work in the first union bakery I ever set foot in. I was puzzled by the fact that young lads were serving four-year apprenticeships to work in bakeries that were so mechanised that skill was done away with. Each time I was sent to work on a chain gang, or to stand for two hours in front of the giant travelling ovens loading on pans, I felt I was becoming like them: robots or, worse still, zombies. I never felt or believed I was a trained baker.

The work was tedious. Each day was a strain. It changed me as a person; I became angry and rebellious, and ended up in many a punch-up.

By the end of my first week I had made a few friends. They were decent, honourable men, and there were many like them in Boland's. I arrived in one morning hurrying along, as I was late. The foreman, Jack, didn't like latecomers, and he swore with a vengeance at them. I detested being late, but it happens. Suddenly I heard a voice calling, 'Paddy, wait.' I looked back, and I saw Jimmy Quinn, heavy-built, with a round fat face, but always with a smile for everyone. 'Hold on, Pat. We're both late – let's go and face him together. Be better that way.' I agreed.

He used the phone inside the hut. I watched as the huge vans and trucks made their way in while Jimmy Quinn could be heard pleading and negotiating our way to work. 'Hello, Jack, Jimmy Quinn and Paddy Touher down below. We're a bit late, Jack.' A long pause. I was astonished at this strange custom, and I felt ashamed that I had fallen so low as to be treated this badly. I was a few minutes late because of the train, but Jimmy and I would be late in joining our shift.

When men didn't show up within ten or fifteen minutes of starting time, the foreman would phone the secretary of the union in the Hall, and if men were available they would be sent out for the day, or longer if they were required. All the union bakeries used jobbers from the Hall. Sometimes a man would be half an hour late, only to find a man in his place when he did arrive, because he didn't phone in to say he'd be late. He would miss a day's work.

Before Jimmy put the receiver down I got a blast of Jack's anger. Jimmy looked me in the eye and said, 'Come on, Pat, we're able for that crap. We're better than that. Jack's just letting off steam, as usual. His bark is worse than his bite.'

I was ending my first month in Boland's when it occurred to me that I hadn't once handled a piece of dough. A record, I thought, for a skilled baker. I was standing with Jim and the Virginian, and I was asked by the foreman what I thought of my first few weeks. I looked him in the eye and said, 'Well, Jack, it's the only bakery I've ever worked in that baked so much and where the bakers touched so little.' I paused a moment then added, 'You know, Jack, I haven't handled a piece of dough yet.'

He smiled. I could see I had touched a nerve. He looked at a man called Mahogany who had sniggered.

'What d'you find so funny? He speaks the truth, yeh mutton-headed fucker.'

I felt sorry for such men, who weren't able to find the words or the courage to speak up for themselves and retain their self-respect against such crude men as Jack – and there were many in the trade who were better suited for an army barracks than a bakery.

Jack was a hard character, though beneath his tough style there was a man I enjoyed having a chat with about the bad old days, when he had men work the shirts off their backs between the old-fashioned Uniflo ovens.

His voice softened and he said, 'So you want to handle up the dough and feel you're a skilled baker?' I nodded and smiled. I looked at the Virginian and Jimmy; both were amused. Jack suddenly pointed at me. 'Okay, show us what you can do and how fast you can do it. If you can mould up the brown sodas over on Wagger's berth, then maybe I'll have sorted a few buggers out at last.'

The Virginian and Jimmy came with me. The Virginian said, 'For fuck's sake, Paddy, you've walked me into this one! You'll have the union on our backs now. It's a showdown!'

The Wagger was a small, middle-aged Dublin man. He always had a pencil stuck behind his ear and a notebook at the ready; he was always taking notes during the day. I began to mould up the sodas. There were now six men around the table. For a while there was silence; then the Wagger shouted, 'Hey, Joxer, I get the feelin' Jack is tryin' to break up the fuckin' berth. What'yeh think?'

Joxer was a very short, stocky man. He moved along the table until he was facing me. I worked the only way I knew how. He noticed I was moulding up quite fast, and it annoyed the rest of the men. Jimmy whispered to me, 'Slow it down, Paddy. Take it easy – union men don't work that way. Slow down or there'll be a bleedin' strike!'

The Wagger shouted, 'Yeh in a fuckin' race, pal?'

I never heard of such talk, and it shocked me. To hell with the whole lot of them, I thought.

The Joxer looked a rough sort, but it was a false image

really. His voice was gruff. 'How yeh.' I nodded and smiled, but kept busy and kept my eyes down. A messy lump of dough landed in front of Mahogany, splashing Joxer with flour in the face. He stopped work and shouted fiercely, 'Who's the bleedin' smart arse? Yeh won't stop the bleedin' berth like that.'

The Wagger added, 'That's right, yeh won't stop the fuckin' train by throwin' dough at a passenger.'

'You're right there, Wagger,' Jack said. 'There's too many fuckin' passengers on this berth.'

After much laughter Jemser said, 'Lookit what yeh started now, Wagger.' I kept working, splitting my sides laughing.

The Joxer got my attention and said, 'What yeh in for, pal, and how'd yeh get here to us?'

I kept my eyes down and gave no response. I noticed that Jack was watching from behind the Joxer. He continued, 'You a jobber or what, or are yeh just passin' by?'

The Wagger was quick off the mark. He shouted, 'The fuckin' sooner he passes by the better, Joxer. I feel like I'm on a bloomin' train up here. You know, pal, I haven't moved as fast since I came back off me honeymoon.'

The men caved in with laughter. Jimmy Quinn glanced at me and winked. I got the message.

The Wagger kept feeding the men with the scaled pieces of brown sodas to be moulded and tinned up by us. He paused to wipe the sweat from his face, whereupon Jack roared out, 'Too hot for yeh, Wagger, is it? Or is our new friend too fast for yez?'

The Wagger's response was fast too. 'Yeh, Jack, I think we'll have to see our shop steward about this one. I get the impression we're on piece work.'

Joxer was only itching to get a word in. 'What non-union hovel did yeh manage to creep out of?'

There was silence now as they all watched me. I knew I had to be careful in my choice of words. Suddenly the Wagger shouted, 'He doesn't bloomin' know, Joxer. He has to feckin' think about it first.'

Joxer responded quickly, looking at me. 'I suppose you're goin' to give us a real fuckin' cock and bull story and treat us like Jack does, like eejits.' I decided to tell them and hope for the best.

'I'm just back from New Zealand, lads. I got a job in the KC, and when the union came up we had to leave. So I'm a jobber now. Okay?'

For a few seconds there was silence, until the little Wagger shouted down at me, 'All the bloomin' way from where?'

The Joxer shouted, 'New Zealand. The other end o' the world, Wagger, to come here to confuse us.' He paused. 'Yeh sure get around, mate. D'yeh mind if I ask yeh how yeh got from down there to here? Enlighten us, will yeh?'

I said, 'I'll try. From Wellington I came through the Magellan Strait, to Santa Cruz in Argentina, on to Buenos Aires ...'

'Argentina, bejapers? Yeh come overland, did yeh?'

I was about to answer when the Wagger got down from his stand, stood at the table and banged it. 'I've got it. He's the Overlander. That's it, men.'

The Wagger and the Joxer stood together, arms around each other, and shouted out, 'Welcome to Boland's, our new friend, the Overlander.'

Jack came across and in his crude way said, 'When you get him noted in your book, Wagger, remember this berth is fucked from now on – broken up. This man can do the work of four men, so from now on you'll have three men with you. Put that in your little black book and remember it.' He laughed as he walked away, rubbing his hands through his white hair.

The Wagger was shouting after him. 'You'll remember the Overlander too, Jack, I promise yeh.'

The Joxer spoke quietly to me. 'Yeh know we mean no harm. The Wagger and me just enjoy a bit o' crack, and we know yeh can take it. See y'around, Overlander. And don't go leavin' us now for the Bridge or some kip.'

Overlander. That name was to stick with me for as long as I found a day's work in a union house.

21

On the last day of 1971 I made my way to the Crystal Ballroom for the New Year's Eve dance. It was my first visit to a ballroom since I returned from New Zealand in the middle of December. I was hopeful of meeting someone, and I felt in the mood the moment I entered the ballroom in Anne Street. Playing that night were my favourite showband: Joe Dolan and the Drifters.

The hall was crowded. Girls I danced with were pushed into me, and I could taste their mascara, lipstick and hair spray all in one. I knew I was home. Once I got among the girls I'd feel smashing. It was their beauty, gaiety and charm that created the atmosphere, along with the chat and the crack. The girls would assemble on one side of the hall, eyeing the male talent on the opposite side, and they would send their signals out to the lads they noticed watching them. Often the men in their haste stampeded across the floor to make sure they got to the girl of their choice.

I met Mando, and we stood on the balcony judging the

form below. I had only one thing on my mind, and that was to get a date or to see some girl home. I looked at my watch and said, 'Damn, I've got less than an hour to make my mark.'

It was great fun asking girls questions as we danced, like 'Do you like the band? Where are you from? Do you like the hall?' and best of all, 'Do you like the floor?' I had a problem in trying to find out exactly where some girls came from. More often than not they would say, 'I'm from the west,' with a total lack of interest, as though they were filling in time. I always got my own back whenever I was asked where I came from by replying, 'I'm from the east!'

Pauline was with two other girls that night as I approached her. I noticed her looking my way, then her smile. The Drifters began to play. I stood near her friend, she said hello, I smiled at her and then at Pauline. I introduced myself and said, 'I hope you're enjoying the dance.' Pauline introduced me to her sister, Anne, and then her friend, who seemed to enjoy looking at me. Then Anne said, 'If you're going to dance, Pat, you'd better hurry up.' She pointed to Pauline. 'That's Joe Dolan who's singing. She's crazy about him.'

Joe Dolan was singing a slow, sexy number. The crowd suddenly stopped dancing for a while to watch their star, as the girls pushed towards the centre of the stage. Many of them were in raptures, screaming for a lock of Joe's hair or to touch his sweaty shirt. I remember looking up to the ceiling and, lo and behold, I realised I was standing right beneath the crystal ball.

When Joe had stopped singing I looked at Pauline. She smiled.

I said, 'You know we are beneath the crystal ball.'

She responded swiftly: 'That's for luck.'

My hands were down by my side; I moved my right hand and suddenly it found hers, waiting to clutch mine. The MC made an announcement: 'Ladies and gentlemen, this spot is two free tickets to next Thursday night's dance. The spot goes to the couple standing beneath the crystal ball.'

'Gosh, we're up!' I said, and I thought of her reply to me moments before, 'That's for luck.' And so it was! As I eased my way up with Pauline to collect the two tickets, I whispered to her, 'It's a date. Okay?' I could tell she was easy-going and jolly, and I liked the way she smiled.

It was the start of something that simply kept going, just as one day follows the next. Joe Dolan was her favourite singing star; Cliff Richard was next, and I came in close, somewhere behind her mother, but I hung in there. It wasn't always easy. Life on the whole is along those lines: a two up and one down sort of way.

I had just moved into new lodgings, but I was beginning

to think that I needed a place of my own. Mrs Megan was a widow, a fine Dublin woman. She certainly knew how to put up a good meal to a hungry lodger. She made the best Dublin coddle I ever had. One evening her words simply swept over me. 'Get your own house, Pat, and find a nice girl to look after it for you. They're building plenty of houses out in Raheny. It's like living in the country, close to the city. You'd be mad not to, Pat. They're going for a song, you know, those houses. That won't always be the case. If I had a lad like you, I'd push you into one of them.'

Mrs Megan poured out the tea. She was curious. 'Have you got a date tonight, Pat?'

Without looking up from the coddle I answered, 'Yes, I have, and before you ask, she's from Dublin.'

I left the house that night feeling terrific. I could feel that change was coming, and for once in my life it felt good. I also realised that it was up to me to make it happen, and to make the right decision for once!

As I drove into the city to pick up Pauline, so many things crossed my mind. I knew I could have been long since married, but it was I who chickened out. I never considered that the girl mightn't have minded if I worked all night and slept all day. I was always afraid of the fact that if I married while I had very low wages and was working odd hours, it would never work out, certainly not how I would like it to.

I had grandiose ideas of what married life should be like, but I was apprehensive about making the big decision.

As I paced up and down the pavement outside McBirney's beside O'Connell Bridge, I was hoping Pauline wouldn't be too late. A baker I worked with came by, known to us as Galway. He shouted, 'Give her up, Paddy. She's not comin'!' I was raging that he knew, and I realised when I'd go into work on the Monday morning I'd be in for a fierce slagging over it, as he'd tell the Wagger and the chain gang.

I waited and waited, and still she didn't come. One bus followed another until eventually I said, 'She'd better be on this one. If she's not then I'm off, and that's it.' If she wasn't on this bus then my decision was made for me, as I detested bad timekeeping. I had been standing for over an hour in the cold. I stopped for a last look, anxiously watching the last person who stepped down from the bus. Never again, I swore, would I go through this waiting for a girl. I put my hands into my pockets and walked away. I heard a voice calling me: it was that baker again. 'Still here, Paddy, yeh feckin' eejit. I told yeh an hour ago I wouldn't wait for my bird like that. Come and have a jar and get the feelin' back into yeh.'

I felt cold, but I said, 'Sorry, I don't drink.'

'What yeh mean yeh don't drink. A baker! You're the only baker I know who doesn't drink.'

I began to walk away, and then I heard a voice calling. 'Pat, wait. Pat, Pat, wait for me.' I could see Pauline hurrying, one hand holding down her brown leather cap. As I walked across O'Connell Bridge I was thinking that only for that young baker meeting me again so suddenly I would have been off, and who knows where I'd have gone!

We used our spot prize won at the Crystal, and as we danced I began teasing her by asking her all the usual questions.

'Do you like Eileen Reid?'

'Yes, do you?'

'Do you like the band? Do you like the Crystal?'

Pauline was quite quick off the mark and responded swiftly, 'Well, do you like the floor, Pat?'

'Yes, I love the floor, and better still, I love those standing on it.'

I could tell Pauline was taken aback. 'Do you mean what you said?'

'Yes, I do, but if you'd behave yourself and turn up on time I'd like you much better.'

She pushed me away from her. 'What! Just who do you think you're talking to? I'm not some girl working in Boland's with that dirty-minded lot, like that baker friend of yours. You don't bring me out to lecture me, even if I was a bit late.'

What have I got here, I wondered! A match, perhaps?

Pauline was a fighter, and would fight her corner. The

coolness of the way she would get out of turning up late and then coolly dress me down often left me gasping. I soon learnt that I could never rely on her punctuality, so I began to drive out to her house and pick her up, which was, I suppose, what she really wanted all the time. I'm a slow learner.

I began to see Pauline three or four times a week. We toured the ballrooms; she was always keen to go to a dance, more so than to see a picture. Sunday nights were reserved for the cinema, and that was that. Pauline had one thing in common with all the other girls I had gone out with: they all got things their own way.

My first invitation to her home was for Sunday dinner. It was a nice spring day, and we could go for a drive to Bray afterwards, I thought. It helped that I was used to staying in lodging houses and having all kinds of landladies to drool over me, so when I entered Pauline's home that first Sunday for dinner I really was at ease with everyone. I arrived early. I had met some of her family on different occasions, but only when picking her up or taking her home; I had never sat down with her parents. I had very little experience of the atmosphere that forms a part of family life.

As I sat down at the table with Tony, Jimmy, Anne and Jimmy's girl-friend, Deirdre, I felt strange. Behaving politely was one thing, but being able to communicate in simple terms was quite another. I got the impression that all was well, though I could feel my every move I made was being scrutinised.

The moment I got home Mrs Megan called out, 'How did you get on, Pat?'

I said, 'Really smashing, great, so it was.'

'You better buy that house, Pat. She's got you, boy. I bet her mother was all over you.'

I smiled at her.

'Your goose is cooked, boy.'

22

I was always apprehensive about owning something new, for fear it would get damaged or stolen. I realised much later it was because as a child I never had much in the way of things such as new toys. Mostly the toys given to us at Christmas were second-hand, or I won them from some other lad in a game of conkers. Whenever I bought something new, be it clothes, shoes, a watch, or perhaps a radio, I took great care of it and had pride in it, as I still do today.

The biggest thing I ever purchased for myself in the first few years after I left school was a new bike, bought in for £17 17s 6d. For the first six months I couldn't stop taking care of it and I was forever polishing it. One day I parked it outside the Catholic Boys' Home for a few minutes; when I came out it was gone. Someone had borrowed it without asking me. The first thought that entered my mind was that I should never have bought a new bike; an old one would have done just as well, and no one would want to steal or borrow it.

I made up my mind that once it was returned I'd sell it and buy a second-hand one.

When I moved towards putting down a deposit on the new house in Grangemore, I worried about all sorts of things. What if the roof blew off in a storm, or it was broken into, or it went on fire? It was only after I had paid my money that my worst fears began to be realised, though I couldn't have made a better move, as time proved. I found it a real headache having so many things to take care of that were never my responsibility before, like changing a light bulb, replacing a fuse, fixing a cracked window, not to mention the upkeep of all interior and exterior painting and decorating, down to doing the garden.

The moment I was handed the key of number 156 Grangemore Estate on that lovely sunny afternoon in June 1972, I felt the weight of the responsibility take precedence over any sense of achievement, and rather than gloat over becoming a member of the home-owners' club, I cast my eyes over the place and said, 'My God, what have I done now!'

I couldn't wait to get up on my bike to get back to collect my gear and say goodbye to my last landlady, the warm-hearted Mrs Megan. 'You'll never make a better move, Pat. May God bless you, son, and look after you. You deserve it.'

I checked again to make certain the belongings were tied

securely on the back. After a few blasts of the horn from the Honda 50, I glanced at Mrs Megan, out at the gate waving, and then I was gone. I wiped the tears away as I turned into Tonelegee Road on the last lap to Raheny.

Within no time I was making my first cup of tea. I had no cooker, just a single gas jet, like the ones we used in the bakery to boil a kettle on. I sat the gas ring into an empty biscuit tin, and connected it to the gas pipe in the kitchen. I spread a tea towel over a couple of cement blocks I rescued from the back garden to use as a table, and sat down on top of another two as a chair.

As I poured the tea I quickly realised there was no milk either. As I stepped out of the front door I met my next-door neighbour. 'Oh, you've just moved in. My name's Kathleen. Pleased to meet you, and so soon too.'

I introduced myself, then I added neatly, 'Sorry, but I've got to run down to the shops for milk: I'm dying for a cup and and it's already made, you see.' Kathleen swiftly dashed into her house and before I could say O'Brien's Bridge she was back holding a bottle of milk, a plate of homemade scones and a cup of sugar. As I tried to take them from her I was afraid she would end up coming in to see how poorly I was set up. Worse luck, I moaned, as she did anyway. 'Oh, goodness, my heavens, you've no furniture!' she cried out, almost dropping the milk.

My first tea set came from Pauline's mother. Each week I would buy one second-hand piece of furniture; each day I dug another bit of the garden. One day to my surprise a van pulled up and my future brother-in-law, Jimmy Brennan, got out to deliver a dining table and four chairs. A terrific feeling came over me with the thought that I was now able to sit at my own table in my own home and have a cup of tea with Pauline, though we were still only engaged.

By the end of the summer in 1972 I had done much to turn the house into a home, with a lot of help from Pauline's mother and father. I had turned the front garden over a few times. One hot, sultry evening I was using a pick, and the sweat was oozing from every part of me. I swung the pick high and brought it down hard. I was shocked to see it suddenly fly from my grasp into the air, then land safely in the soil.

Just then my future father-in-law walked up the drive with Pauline, followed by Jimmy. Jimmy looked at me in amazement. 'What happened? I saw the pick take off.'

I looked down at the plastic pipe it had hit. 'Look,' I said. 'Down here, Jim.' He was shocked. He shouted, 'Good God, Pat, you're lucky to be alive. You hit the electric cable.' As we entered the house Jimmy turned to me and said, 'For Christ's sake, Pat, you must have nine lives. You were born lucky.'

But then his father raised his voice and said, ''Tis not luck at all, Jim: sure he's blessed.' He looked at me and added, 'You must have said your prayers this morning.' I was pleased by Pauline's interruption: 'He's fine. You know, Father, he's only a baker. He wouldn't have much time at half four in the mornings to pray. He couldn't think straight at that unholy hour.'

At last the day of the wedding was set: 10 February 1973; and as each week passed a little bit more was done to the house. I had bought some carpets, and when they were put down I was in great humour. I looked around the empty rooms with Pauline and said, 'Isn't it beautiful? Everything matches up just lovely. All we need now, Pauline, is the furniture!'

She smiled in her attractive way and said, 'There's much more to life, Pat, than fancy tables and cosy chairs, you know.'

I was startled at that, after thinking about all I had done. I didn't think that Pauline might have other priorities. Our relationship was on the rocky side yet we loved each other. Money was so scarce it made life difficult. Pauline had walked out on me on several occasions over what she called my dominant ways. Her mother often remarked how I marched into the house, and through life on the whole, like a soldier. 'You should calm down, Pat, and take it easy, son.'

As the time drew near I began to question whether I should get married at all. I wondered how I could settle down to a home life, and be a father, perhaps. I became tense and acted in a rather irritated manner towards Pauline and those I worked with. I was steadily getting used to living alone in my own home, which was bad, as the longer a person lives alone the harder it is to adjust when they get married. I found it tough going getting the house furnished and paying all the bills on a very low wage.

It was a smashing August evening as I ambled in from work to find a letter waiting for me. I rarely received post, and as I opened it I realised it was from Pauline. I could feel the tension mount. I went up to my bedroom to lie down to read it. After the first few lines I felt choked, and by the time I reached its conclusion I was disappointed and confused. Now what is she playing at? So she needs time to think, a few weeks. Well, she can have as long as she wants!

I stood at the window staring out. My mind was flooded with the memory of the many times I was close to getting married only to see it all crumble, for one reason or another, and now again! What had I done to deserve this?

I was fed up with my lifestyle. Getting up at four in the morning, getting to Boland's Bakery by 5.45am, not getting home until 6pm. I was jaded, tired. In fact I hated my life so much I was tempted to return to New Zealand. But I loved Pauline.

'Things will get better. It takes time to get it together when you move into a new house,' Mrs Megan explained. 'You've got the house, Pat, and the girl and a beautiful one she is. Take my advice and marry her.'

I decided to go for a walk. I stared out across the sea, thinking what a fool I'd been, and as I gazed out to the horizon I got a longing to get on board a liner and go around the world without ever getting off. I knew that Pauline was right to take her time, and that she could have all the time she needed to decide whether she wished to marry me or to simply say goodbye. I knew I had found a woman worth waiting for. And I made up my mind that if she broke it off, I would set off for distant shores.

One evening I travelled home by train. As I walked through Donaghmede Shopping Centre I was stopped by two Christian Brothers whom I instantly recognised from my time in Artane, Brother Crowe and Brother Monaghan. I was surprised to discover how young they looked. Both were anxious to know what my opinion was of Artane School. Though I was taken by surprise with their questions, and unprepared, I decided to answer them frankly.

'On the whole I'd say it was an endurance test. As each day began I feared so much, most of all the hard men. It was an experience more than an education.'

I tried my best to sum up for them what they were capable

of and what they were good at doing. I said, 'Education is not a trial, Brothers. In Artane you were all part of a system. The system came first, and you were masters at how to make the harsh system work and to make us suffer.'

Their expressions hardened. Brother Monaghan smiled and said, 'Please go on, though I hope you can explain as well what we were good at.'

''Tis a shame the Brothers had to act so cruelly for minor faults. Education is not about how hard or disciplined you are or how you keep order. I believe it is all about learning in easy stages, to help the child's mind to develop. I believe the system you helped to develop only helped to destroy a lot of the good things you were doing; and without those hard leathers in the classrooms I would honestly say that the Christian Brothers would have achieved the highest standards, which you were indeed capable of.'

As I went to move away Brother Crowe called after me. 'Did we fail you, Pat?'

That was an easy one, I thought. 'No, no, the system left its mark on me, and though it certainly held me back in an educational sense, remember I was a duffer. I also believe that the Brothers were struggling to do their best for us, and there were so many of us. Yet when I left, it was a real struggle to come to terms with the emotional aspect of leaving such a strict institution, which I lived under for so long.'

'So what you are saying is that you weren't fully prepared for the outside world.'

'And I suffered so much awful abuse! 'Twas a pity you had to be so cruel. The punishment was never justified, particularly in the classrooms and dormitories.'

I was unprepared for this, I thought, as Brother Monaghan drew closer to me, his face flushed. 'So, we were cruel and used physical force. Tell me, how else could less than 100 Brothers keep strict control of 900 boys? Many of those boys were tough and streetwise, Pat.'

I replied, 'In all my eight years, there was always about 400–500 from the country. We were all treated in the same brutal manner for very trivial and silly offences. Fear was the key of keeping strict rigid control.'

'But no other system could have achieved that result,' said Brother Monaghan. Brother Crowe nodded in full agreement with his long-time friend.

'No other system was ever tried in my eight years of prayer, hard labour and physical punishment and widespread abuse, and both of you were there in most of my time ... Though ye treated me fine as I recall.'

That brought a smile to their tanned faces, and as I went to go on my way Brother Monaghan said, 'Take care, Collie.' Brother Crowe seemed curious and asked, 'What brought you this way?'

I smiled and said, 'Well, I've bought a house just up the road there.'

'Ah, well done, boy, a home of your own. You've come a long way!'

As I stepped it out swiftly through the crisp autumn leaves I paused to watch young children playing conkers, which brought back emotional memories to my busy mind. But my thoughts quickly changed as I walked home to my own house with its own table and chairs and a bed where I could dream.

23

One beautiful autumn evening in 1972 I walked into the hall and saw a letter on the floor. A quick glance told me it was from Pauline. I was invited over to her house for dinner the following Sunday.

I was warmly greeted by Pauline's mother. 'Come in, you're most welcome, son.' Within moments I was being hugged and kissed by Pauline in the narrow hall. By the time Sunday dinner was over I felt I was part of the family.

I could see the change in Pauline. She had made her decision and was keen to go ahead with the wedding, and we began to make the arrangements.

We got married on 10 February on a clear, crisp Saturday. As I stood on the steps of the church in Marino, I wished all my old Artane pals could see me now: Quickfart, Minnie, Jamjar, the Skunk, the Burner. I took my seat and I whispered to the best man, my good friend Tony Lally from Ballybough, 'Do you think she'll come?' He looked at me and laughed.

'Don't worry, Paddy, she'll come, but it might take a while.'

I wondered why he thought it was so funny.

My baker friend from Boland's pleased the hearts of all the congregation with his beautiful deep baritone voice as he sang 'Lord of All Hopefulness', my favourite recessional hymn, while everyone awaited the arrival of the bride. He followed this with 'Ave Maria' as the bells rang to announce Pauline's arrival.

'She finally arrives,' said Father Dermot O'Mahony, with a nice smile. Pauline was always late for every occasion.

After the ceremony we set off from the airport on our honeymoon: two weeks in El Arenal, Spain.

It took me a long time to get used to the fact that I was married. I had no inkling of the number of difficulties I had to face in the sudden change from being single, and being able to please myself about whatever I wanted to do, to being a married man and having to learn to share myself and my time and to relate to my wife as my partner.

I was exhausted coming home from Boland's, and became a real mixture of all sorts. I wasn't able to understand Pauline's problems, and there were problems from the day we crossed the threshold in the house in Grangemore Estate.

Pauline was pleasant and easy-going, as she remained for the rest of her life. Thank goodness for that, as I was so domesticated and dominant. My concept of marriage was very different from hers. I believed in the old style: my wife would be waiting with my dinner cooked, and a smile, as I came in from another hard day at work. But to my amazement I would arrive home to find a note saying, 'Dear Pat, As you could be out all hours and as you yourself don't very well know what time you'll be home at, I'm at Mother's and I will have my dinner there.'

Once I got over the shock of her not being at home, I'd swear under my breath at the way she would sign off the note

with, 'Good luck, you can help yourself, Love, Pauline.'
Help myself? I wasn't fit to stand up when I got in after being
out from before five in the morning. I'd laugh at the whole
idea of her 'take it easy' style and 'don't worry'. This kind of
situation in a newly married's home is fun for television
viewers, but it's not funny in reality to stare into an empty
fridge or to put on the kettle for a cup of tea only to find
there's no milk.

After a few weeks I began to realise that there was a lot
more to being married than I had imagined. I was soon to
come face to face with hurt of a different kind, as I discovered when, on arriving in from work, I might pass some
remark more suitable for the chain gang in Boland's than for
the sensitive ears of my wife. Even when I'd only mutter or
grumble a harsh remark, though it wouldn't seem harsh to
me, she would pick it up. Soon I discovered that I couldn't
behave as though I was coming home to the lads in the
Catholic Boys' Home; and yet as I would hear the door slam
I would say to myself, 'Good God, what have I done now?
Ah, sure I just said the wrong thing.' I'd laugh at my simple
explanation.

I believe after all these years of trial and error that she was
right in many ways and I was wrong. I was far too domesticated for Pauline: I always had to be doing something or
other, like tidying, cleaning the windows, dusting everything,

while she was only concerned with watching her favourite programme on television. What surprised me was that she would never thank me for doing a good job in the house or in the garden. I'd march in feeling great and say, 'Thank God that's done.' She'd simply say, 'Good for you, Pat. What do you expect, some kind of payment?'

Ten months passed when our first child, Paula, was born in December 1973, one week before our first Christmas together.

On a cold crisp day in January 1974, our firstborn was christened by our parish priest. Pauline couldn't agree on a name after weeks thinking on it. At that time, we called my wife Paula. It was the priest, Father O'Mahony, who came up with the solution. 'Why not call the baby Paula, and you can refer to your wife as Pauline.' So our firstborn was christened and baptised Paula Ann Touher.

The experience made a huge change to my marriage; it tied me down and made me a better person. Just one year later we had the best New Year's present we could have hoped for when John Patrick was born.

While Paula had her baby brother to keep her occupied, Pauline was constantly busy with the two children. Money was tight: every last penny I could earn was needed in the home and we never had enough. But we were happy together.

Being a dad and devoted husband to Pauline gave me a real sense of well being and satisfaction. At last I felt normal!

The summer of 1975 was one to remember. I was more or less putting up with my lot as a baker, working long hours, getting up before dawn and getting home after dark. I longed to write; but when I came home and sat down to discuss my dreams with Pauline, she would only encourage me to go up to bed and do my dreaming there!

I began to get some encouragement to write about my childhood. While I was in Boland's I had heard the men say whenever Artane School was mentioned that a book should be written on that place. The more I heard it said the more inspired I'd become, only to find myself too tired to think, let alone write.

In August I was out in the front garden. The sun was high, the sky was blue and cloudless, and I was leaning on the wooden fence when I heard a van pull up. A man got out and walked towards me. 'I'm looking for Pat, he's a baker. I think it's Touher or something like that.'

I said, 'You've found him. What can I do for you?' He reached out his hand and introduced himself.

'I'm Jimmy Mack. How would you like to come back to work and manage the home bakery for us? We need a good man who knows his job and who's the best at the soda bread.

The hours are 10am to finish around four or so.' I gasped, wow!

I agreed to go down to the bakery in Windsor Avenue in Fairview and talk to the boss. I knew Jim Behan well, as I had worked with him and for him in Bradley's when he took it over. I liked him and his family. I had fond memories of the days I went out to his mother's in Bray to help with the harvest, which brought back memories of my own childhood in Barnacullia.

For the next six years I managed the bakery with the help of Ken Quinn. I was back at the bakery I had first worked in after I left Artane, when Mick Bradley was my boss.

I began to enjoy work, as I was at the heart of things in Behan's Home Bakery, back to my roots. I had moved from Grangemore to Woodville Estate in Coolock, and whether by luck or by error I discovered I was back in full view of Artane School and that I would be passing it every day of the week. I saw quite a lot of the Macker and his colleagues around the area.

24

At this time, the turn of the eighties, I was doing reasonably well in work and in my marriage. Pauline and I were a real item and I loved her so. I was leading a normal life with a beautiful wife and two children in school, and another on the way. However, when Pauline told me that the children would have to move on to more senior schools a change loomed. The road for John would lead straight back to my past. John would have to attend St David's National School, which would prepare him for St David's Seniors – what in my day had been Artane Industrial School. When we told John he cried and cried, and Pauline and I decided to move far away from the bleak, grey stone, haunting buildings that cast their long, dark shadow over our lives. The search for our new home and a new job was completed just as Suzanne, our third child, entered the world. It turned out to be a very inspiring move to the seaside town of Balbriggan.

*

It was about 1979 that my friend Ken Quinn talked me into doing a soccer referees' course under Kevin Redmond and Tommy Hand. I was none too keen. Since I was a child I've had a phobia about written tests or exams. At first I dismissed the idea; then I began to see myself out on the pitch among twenty-two players, running with them, enjoying one of the greatest field games in the world. A feeling of warm excitement began to grip me.

The referees' course turned out to be a most enjoyable experience. I met people who were just as scared of written tests as I was, but the inspectors and committee members from the Irish Soccer Referees' Society went out of their way to make the course run as smoothly as possible for us all. The chief inspector at that time was Kevin Redmond, and he was my guiding light. His relaxed manner ensured that every one of the class had a comfortable passage through the short course.

The more forceful characters, like Sean Fitzpatrick, Albert Walsh and the driving force behind the Dublin branch of the Referees' Society, Tommy Hand, lectured us constantly on the rules of the game until we were ready to scream 'foul'. It was men like them and, later, the calming influence of big Willy Attley that ensured the course was a success. With their help we became good referees. It was their untiring and devoted work that had brought the Irish Referees' Society to the top.

I was given no less than three match cards for my first weekend. Kevin Redmond signed the cards for me and said, 'Follow the simple rules, Pat, and you won't go far wrong. Treat the players as you would wish to be treated if you were a player. Don't be rude to them, or to the team managers. Turn up well before kick-off. Dress neatly, and don't act like a dominant schoolmaster. Simply go out there and enjoy what you're doing.'

I followed Kevin's advice for twenty-five years.

I will always remember my first match as a soccer referee. It was out in Collinstown, near Dublin Airport, on a Saturday afternoon. Fenstanton were at home to Whitehall Rangers. Instead of measuring the balls in the dressing room, I decided to check them on the pitch, as the teams had changed outside because the weather was so hot. I had a piece of string with me that I had measured before I left home; I had a knot tied in each end of it, and from one knot to the other measured twenty-eight inches, just as Kevin Redmond had instructed us on the course.

I felt really important as the manager of Fenstanton came up to me while I was checking the nets. 'How'yeh, ref? Here's the match balls. I suppose you want to check them as well.'

I glanced across to the touch-line and noticed that Pauline and her father, Tony, were in fits of laughter. As I began to measure one of the balls I could hear them laughing even louder and, like a fool, wondered why. Suddenly I heard a

shout from one of the Rangers' players: 'Are you all right, ref?'
I instantly looked up and responded briefly, 'Sure. Why do
you ask?' There was no response. I noticed that the players
were having a good laugh, so I began to put my piece of string
around the second ball, as I was not happy with the pressure
in the first one. Just as I completed my check I was
approached by the Fenstanton manager. He spoke hurriedly,
though struggling to remain serious I thought. 'What's up, ref?
Yeh got a problem?' I answered sharply: 'No, not at all. I'm
just measuring the balls. I like this one.' As he took the ball
some of the players shouted to him, 'What's up, boss?' He
shouted back, 'Nothing. The ref was just measuring his balls.'

Football – soccer – was forbidden by the Christian Brothers
as it was an English game. Any boys caught playing it would
have their arses beaten off them. And yet, after I left Artane,
I grew to love the game. I went to see Manchester United at
Old Trafford and I supported my home team whenever I
could. I love football, and I loved my time as a referee.
Standing in a middle of a pitch, surrounded by twenty-two
young players, all playing their hearts out, there were times
when I wished that the Christian Brothers could see me now.
They failed to beat the love of the sport out of me, just as they
had failed to break my spirit.

25

In 1985 I found myself out of work, which was very unusual for me. However, around that time I began once again to have a burning desire to write my story of growing up in Artane Industrial School. But the big problem for me was I had no idea how to write a book even though I had great faith in myself that I would be able to do it.

I remember unloading the car and saying to myself, 'I'll have the script written by Christmas if I get stuck into it, and write at least ten pages per day, five days a week,' as on Saturdays and Sundays I was involved in soccer as a referee. Things were going along so well at last I could see the wood for the trees. The story was really taking shape and it was ringing true. The characters were really touchable and human, unlike in all my previous scripts. I began to enjoy the whole experience of writing for myself; to tell a story that I believed had to be told.

One day, when I was busy working on my story, my daughter Paula came in with a letter addressed to me that had just arrived in the post. I opened it immediately, Pauline reading it over my shoulder. It was an invitation to attend an interview at the Beaumont Hospital, which had just opened. It was a temporary position as a ward attendant; it wasn't something that I had any experience in, but still, it was a job.

Paula asked me if I would take it if it were offered to me. Pauline drew closer to me to encourage me. 'Go for it, Pat. It could be a great help to you, you know.'

I looked up at her: she was smiling. The late August sun was strong that afternoon and Paula's long red hair glowed. She was only fourteen, but wiser than her years and very studious. 'You're not going for another temporary job again are you? You will never finish that story if you keep taking on Mickey Mouse jobs. Someone out there might beat you to it, then your story will be useless.'

My heart sank, but Paula was right. Thoughts of someone else getting a book published on Artane before my own was finished drove me to get on with it.

However, Pauline was keen I went for the position, and I decided that August day to go for the interview. The fact was, I needed to work, as much for my own sense of self-worth as for the money, but I knew I could and would write my story even if I had to remain up until the early hours every morning.

That Friday I went to the Beaumont Hospital for an interview. I was shown to a small, drab office where I was asked to fill in a form while I waited for my interview. Name, address, phone number – that was easy. I paused when it asked my date of birth and where I was born. Was it the city centre, Dominick Street or perhaps in Westland Row? I smiled as I put down 'City Centre'. I had to pause again as I came to the next question. Father's name? Mother's maiden name? Even though it had been almost forty years since I went to Artane, still the facts of my birth came back to haunt me. I was sure that it was all a cod, and I would not be employed, not even temporarily.

I was interviewed by a well-rounded Matron who wore a nice smile. She spoke awfully grand, 'How do you do, I'm the sister in charge of Adams O'Connell,' and after that I became lost in a world which was far removed from that from which I had just come.

I was not at all sure where I stood. Suddenly she got down to brass tacks, and I was relieved, but mostly surprised. 'Are you available to start work on Monday, Patrick? I hope you are not the squeamish type, as you will be required to help the nurses on the wards with bathing, dressing and lifting the patients.'

She reminded me of Bridget Doyle in Barnacullia.

As I drove home I was in two minds. My daughter's words came hammering at me: 'You'll never ever complete the script, Dad, if you take a Mickey Mouse job.' I felt like turning the car around and telling them to find someone else. But the other side of me would not let me do that. The work ethic that the Christian Brothers beat into me became my strength that made me determined to work hard and to aim for success.

I believe that the time that I worked in the neurosurgical ward of the new Beaumont Hospital certainly helped me a great deal. Each evening as I sat down to write, often writing until two in the morning, the flow began to come and I began to write not fully knowing where to stop. I began to believe in myself at last. I felt inspired by working with the sick; I was glad to be able to help them.

Many patients I worked with had undergone brain surgery, and it was part of my duties to help the nurses feed these patients, to wash, shave and shower them. There was many an occasion when I very much had to take a deep breath and grin and bear it. It was often very difficult to see these pour souls suffering, but I tried my hardest to help the nurses make them comfortable. It was a whole new experience for me.

Nevertheless it was a huge relief to get home from the hospital and sit down to write. The will to succeed was extremely strong within me, and in fact the hospital work was very therapeutic. Soon I was beginning to see my story taking shape.

As I was writing by hand it was slow progress and after many drafts decided it was time to look for a typist and make a start in getting the first few chapters typed up. Yet I couldn't come up with the right name. 'Artane – the True Story' didn't quite get across what my story was about. My search for a more powerful and imaginative title began as there is so much in a name.

One late October evening, tired from writing, I decided to meander out by the sea, determined to return with the new exciting title. My mind went to work as I strolled by the railway line. As I came towards the bridge I could see the tall trees silhouetted against the late autumn sky and, nestling behind them, the grey stone beauty of Saint George's church close to the railway line. Its tall spire has become a famous landmark pointing to the heavens.

Arriving home that night I still hadn't come up with the right title. I wrote down a list of all the titles I had thought up. All of them began with the word 'Fear'. And as I went through the list with my family after tea that night, 'Fear of the Collar' was the only one that everyone liked.

But even though I finally had the right title, I suddenly realised that evening how behind I was with my education. I had given my children everything that I lacked. They were so far ahead of me in modern life and learning. They studied Shakespeare and Arthur Miller at school; my days were filled with hard labour, prayer and punishment. I was proud of them, but daunted with the writing process ahead of me.

While I was writing *Fear of the Collar* my nightmares came back and I was talking in my sleep. This was clearly linked to the writing process, and reliving memories that I had tried to suppress for years. I found it was a most difficult task, to sit down until two or three in the morning, tearing up much of what I'd written on previous occasions, to replace it with better material. The shadow of Artane School, and its harsh military-style system, took over my whole mind, body and soul. I'd go to bed exhausted and within moments I'd enter my dark childhood back in Artane.

I was having some awful dreams of the Apeman beating dozens of us boys, all naked and lined up with our hands joined as though we were praying for mercy. For some unknown reason I'd wake up when my turn came to be flogged by the Christian Brothers. I was often writing about Driller the Killer on duty in the shower rooms. Once I dreamt that I was Driller the Killer. I marched the seventh and eighth division, all naked, from the snow-covered parade ground. I was standing on a wooden platform shouting, 'Left, left, lift them up, left right left.' As I marched the two naked divisions into the showers, we met up with the Artane band marching out, playing the 'Bold Fenian Men'. The boys got so excited I began to flog each one of them while the band kept on playing. I woke drenched in perspiration.

'You've been at it again, Pat,' said a smiling Pauline.

I felt embarrassed. 'What do you mean?'

'Shouting orders in your sleep. I was one of your dirty

pups and you actually ordered me to bend over and touch me toes. And I had to take off my night-shirt. Imagine that now.'

'What did you do?' I was in fits laughing.

'It's a good job it was for boys only.' Her smile was so radiant, and always tempting …

Writing *Fear of the Collar* was in a real sense having to relive my eight years all over again. The fact that I was dreaming and talking in my sleep simply confirmed to me that I was telling the real facts. But I made the decision not to reveal the full horrors of the systematic sexual and physical abuse I suffered inside. I wanted to save my wife and our three young children the embarrassment I believed it would cause them.

That decision I made back then turned out to be the correct one for all of us in the family, particularly the children. Furthermore, whenever I made an effort to describe in detail the form or methods employed by the Christian Brothers who performed such acts of sexual and physical abuse on us, it was indeed way beyond my station back then. As it was, I was finding it a very difficult task to write down the basics and to get my story told. As I write this at the end of 2007 I find it is less stressful.

It took me four years to write *Fear of the Collar*, and while I was worried about another ex-Artaner telling his story before me, I was anxious to get the facts straight. When I felt that my story was ready to go into the world, I started to approach Irish publishers. I anxiously awaited the postman, fearful of rejection, though at the same time realising that many successful authors had been rejected more than once before they had their work accepted.

I will never forget that evening in November 1990 when I contacted O'Brien Press. I was amazed to hear that the editor had been meaning to contact me about it, and although there were a few other publishers interested, I thought I had found the right one in O'Brien Press.

When I set out to write my story I did so for a few particular reasons. One was that I believed I had a good story to tell, which I knew had to be told. I had prayed to God that I would be the one to tell it. I was of the opinion that it needed to be told and in a balanced way, and that I was the one to tell it. I'm so glad I'm still writing to this very day. 'Tis hard to believe it really, particularly with my lack of education. As I look back to the beginning, in 1985 to 1989, Pauline was always there to give me encouragement and help. I was blessed I had such a beautiful and devoted wife, as Pauline was, to be there for me. As it was such a very difficult story for me to explain in great detail I doubt I'd have made it without her. She was my light and she gave me hope, and the will to succeed in revealing the dark secret of my stolen childhood. Pauline was as surprised as anyone on hearing of my secret past.

26

It was September 1998. A beautiful time of the year, September, when the corn is ripened gold. The countryside is rich in colour, mellow dark yellow, rustic and gold. I love the scent and warmth of autumn as I did as a child when I lived in the cottage home of my dreams in the hillside of Barnacullia in Sandyford, south county Dublin.

For me, those fond and cherished memories were indeed happy and carefree, growing up in Barnacullia in the hillside and going to school in Sandyford. And returning home through the fields and leafy glades, and filling our pockets with shiny mahogany-coloured conkers, a sign that autumn is here for certain.

That autumn I decided to take Pauline and our youngest daughter Suzanne to the Algarve. Suzanne was extra excited because we had agreed that she could take a schoolfriend, Silvie, with her. Once we arrived in the Algarve, we were knocked by the heat – it was at least thirty-five degrees Celsius.

To my astonishment I began to feel as though I'd found I had energy to burn. We agreed to let the girls go off together to fun parks, water worlds and that sort. That allowed Pauline and I to travel and explore places like Lagos, Alvor, Rio Lobo and Monechoro. Though it was mid-September the temperature was reaching heights of almost forty degrees.

But although Pauline was having a wonderful time, and fell in love with the old town of Portimao, and Lagos in particular, I couldn't help but feel uneasy about her, especially when the evening closed in. Dancing in the open air on sultry evenings overlooking the great long, golden, sandy beach below which hundreds of couples chatted and drank Sangria and wine, I began to notice a sudden change in my wife. Though I could feel it, and see it, I couldn't quite put my finger on what was wrong. She would cling to me as we walked, danced or simply just stood gazing at the wonderful beauty of the Algarve at night. Pauline was holding on to me as though she might fall if I let go.

On the few occasions I ventured to ask her whether she was okay, her instant brilliant smile quite simply helped to alleviate my concerns for a while. Though I was concerned I didn't let my concerns spoil the holiday. Pauline looked great, more attractive than ever, and her smile became even more radiant.

I noticed that Pauline was dragging her left foot. Her shoe was so worn down on the heel, it became very noticeable. I was very concerned, though I had no idea as to what was the cause of it. Never once did I hear Pauline ever complain.

A few days after we returned from Portugal, when I got home from work Suzanne told me that her mother had fallen over again. I was stunned. 'What do you mean by "again"?' I asked my youngest child.

Suzanne's expression was one filled with apprehension as she told me it was about the fifth time Pauline had fallen since we returned from the Algarve. We stared at each other for an empty, silent, awful moment. Suzanne was worried about her, but didn't want her mum to know that she had told me about her falls.

Pauline was never one to complain, and hated the embarrassment it would have caused her, so it wasn't until a few days later, when we were having a drink in the pub, that I asked her how her ankle was. When she looked at me, her voice was soft. 'Oh, so you've noticed after all.'

'Yes, in fact I'm quite concerned. Have you been to the doctor?'

'Yes, I've to have it X-rayed soon. I was told to go to the Lourdes Hospital.' Later that evening at home I had a look at Pauline's foot and suddenly feared something was very wrong here. It's very blue, very stiff, no movement. 'How does it affect you, is there any pain?' I asked her.

She kept smiling at me. 'No, none. I just find it's not normal, it's so stiff and very dead.' We had to put our trust in the hospitals now. But we were soon to realise that was a big mistake.

Despite going to both the Lourdes and Mater hospitals, nothing could be found. But I knew something was wrong. Being involved in soccer, having to keep fit, gave me the gut feeling something was very wrong. I was very concerned.

It was late in the evening towards the end of November. I was in the sitting room watching TV. I heard a commotion, screams. Pauline was lying on the floor. 'She just fell over, Dad. She was talking to us,' Suzanne said.

I looked down at Pauline sitting on the kitchen floor. I was amazed that she was smiling. 'Can you do anything to help Mam?' Suzanne pleaded.

'Come on Pauline, let me lift you up,' I said. As I carried her in my arms to the sitting room, her spontaneous burst of laughter filled the house. God, how I loved her.

The next morning I drove Pauline to our doctor's surgery. The surgery was in a beautiful old red-bricked Victorian style. I helped Pauline out of the car. Our eyes met. 'Are you worried?' I asked.

She simply looked at me and said, 'I leave all the worrying to you, Pat. Let's go inside.'

I certainly felt nervous as I entered the doctor's office. 'Hello Pauline, let me take your coat and hat.' I watched Dr Alan gently help Pauline off with her coat. He wanted to examine Pauline in private, so I left the office to wait.

Finally, the door opened; the doctor's voice was very soft. 'Patrick, it's not good news, I'm afraid. I will need to refer Pauline to a specialist to be sure, but it seems to be that she could be suffering from MS.'

Dr Alan explained multiple sclerosis to me as a highly individual experience for every different person with the disease. He warned me that Pauline could be confined to a wheelchair, but that that would depend on what form of MS she had.

We were referred to Dr Orla Hardiman, a consultant neurologist at the Beaumont Hospital Clinic, where I had worked as a porter all those years ago. But before then was Christmas, and, as usual, Paula and John came to stay. As I watched the gifts being unwrapped I kept my eye on Pauline. If she had a serious problem, then she was doing a remarkable job at hiding it from us. Not for a mere brief moment did any of us think that this was to be the last Christmas dinner we'd enjoy together with Pauline.

Ten weeks later the family had gathered around Pauline's bedside to hear the worst possible news. Paula and John sat close together while Suzanne sat close by her mother's side. Pauline had a very aggressive form of Motor Neurone Disease, or MND, and her prognosis was bleak. I stared at the consultant in disbelief as we were told the news that MND is incurable and fatal. We were told that Motor Neurone Disease is not contagious, nor is it an inherited condition. Nobody knows for certain why one person contracts it and another doesn't. Many sufferers may have had it for most of their lives before it took hold. The consultant told us how sorry she was, but Pauline was unlikely to survive the year.

It was as if the sky had fallen in on me. We were told by the doctor that all we could do for Pauline was to care for her needs in a gentle, loving way, but since the Beaumont was a recovery hospital, it was not possible that Pauline could stay, as her condition was non-recoverable. But nor should Pauline return home. In fact, the best place for her was a nursing home, where she would receive quality of life and round-the-clock care. It was explained to me that it was going to be very difficult for me to give Pauline the kind of care she needed.

But Pauline wanted to stay at home. So against the advice given to me by the doctors and nursing care team at the Beaumont, and the IMNDA – the Irish Motor Neurone Disease Association, I stood by Pauline and her wish to be taken home. As far as I was concerned Pauline was now the only person in the world that really mattered. Once I got Pauline home everything simply fell into place. Suzanne was wonderful. Every day when she would return home from school, her voice would ring out, 'Hello Mam, Mam, I'm home. Dad with you, Mam?' We were helped enormously by the IMNDA, who brought us a bed that would put Pauline in a sitting position at the touch of a button, a chair, a hoist and they organised some home help for us.

The disease progressed rapidly. It was now April. I heard from a friend in Balbriggan town that there was a trip to Lourdes going out in May. I couldn't wait to get home to Pauline to tell her the news. 'How would you like to go to Lourdes?' Tears of joy swept down her flushed cheeks. Her voice was soft, very soft. 'Love it, love it.' Though I didn't expect a miracle, Lourdes gave Pauline a wonderful lift. It raised her spirits and kept her smile radiant to the end.

Pauline's condition worsened every week. As the dreadful disease attacked, Pauline's speech became slurred. The movement in her left hand died slowly as time passed agonizingly by.

In the early hours of the morning I'd be shaken out of a deep sleep by the sound of the buzzer. I'd go to the fridge, take out a tray of ice cubes and smash them with a hammer wrapped in a tea towel. Pauline's eyes would simply light up. Her smile widened. 'Ah, lovely, lovely, lovely,' she'd murmur with some effort, at the cool taste of the water.

It was after our visit to Lourdes that I began to receive much-needed help. The Balbriggan Clinic and Medical Centre sent nurses as Pauline required twenty-four-hour care. Pauline and I were also very pleased with the voluntary care from Ann Walsh, Rita McCormack, next-door neighbour Lorraine and Alice Crowe, Sylvie's mum. Sylvie was Suzanne's closest pal along with Gayle and Sandra, who gave Suzanne so much support.

The weekends became a real treat for Pauline as the whole family came, although sometimes it could be over-whelming as everyone tried to help. Pauline's sister Ann, brothers Tony and Jim, and mother May would sit in the garden in the summer of 1999 and soak in the breeze. Paula, John and Suzanne would also come over and take their mother out in the wheelchair, especially so she could admire the colours of autumn. They would take her by the cliffs, by old Fancourt along the Bower, for her to gaze fondly at the Mourne Mountains and to watch the most colourful old fishing boats return to the ancient Balbriggan harbour. For Pauline, the weekends couldn't come too soon.

I was amazed at Pauline's courage. Motor Neurone Disease, once it takes hold, is a slow, painful death without relief and without hope. But sometimes Pauline's smile would make me forget that her days on the earth were numbered.

Each morning I would climb out of bed to the sound of the doorbell. Sleepily I would make my way to let the nurse in to see to Pauline. Anne would prepare Pauline, give her a check over, then give her a shower, wash her hair. She loved being nursed by Anne. I assisted the nurse in every way I could.

One morning, over a cup of tea, Nurse Anne told me that she had noticed Pauline's condition worsen, and that – as I had been with her constantly, day and night I probably didn't realise just how bad she was. In fact, Nurse Anne believed that Pauline had to be moved to the hospice for twenty-four-hour care. Still I stood by Pauline: she didn't want to leave her home, and I had to give her this final promise, for as long as I could.

The celebration of the Mass in our home by our dear friend Bishop Dermot O'Mahony and Father Michael Carey near the end of October 1999 lifted Pauline's spirits, though before everyone arrived Pauline, for some unknown reason, cried rivers. I was baffled as Suzanne tried everything to calm her mum by brushing her hair and doing her make-up till at last Pauline smiled. Folk began to arrive for the service: the choir arrived with all their instruments, the nurses and doctors, family and close friends all seemed to arrive en masse until our home was bursting at the seams.

I had known Father Dermot O'Mahony for years. He was, in many ways, a modern-day priest, young, lively and willing to help. He wasn't afraid to get in among people in the communities to help them. His was an out-going, charismatic personality, and a breath of fresh air. He performed the wedding service for Pauline and me in 1973. He christened our first child and he always seemed to be there when First Holy Communions came along. As the children got older he was at St Peter's and Paul's in Balbriggan for their Confirmations. On the night of 20 October 1999, Dermot was present once again to celebrate Mass, and then once more on All Souls' Day to give the last rites to Pauline.

While the girls from the Community College sang '*Cead Mile Failte Romhat*' my thoughts travelled back to when I first met Pauline at a New Year's Eve Ball in the Crystal Ballroom in 1971. As the north wind blew in carrying mist from the sea the Lone Piper stood by our home in the Cove. 'Amazing Grace' filled the cold November damp air as they carried Pauline's remains to the waiting funeral car.

The piper solemnly played the hauntingly beautiful 'My Lagan Love' as we slowly walked the half mile to the chapel to be met by hundreds of school children dressed in their uniforms. They walked slowly and silently in solemn respect to honour one of their own. The end comes like dust on the wind: like the fallen leaf can never be replaced what's gone, is gone for ever.

27

On a warm summer's day in May of 1999 the prime minister, the Taoiseach Mr Bertie Ahern, made a public apology to all survivors of child abuse in semi-state run institutions, such as convents, boarding schools run by the clergy, and Christian Brothers boys' industrial schools in Ireland from the 1940s to the 1970s and beyond.

Later, in 2000, that apology was followed up by one by the late Pope John Paul II for all the sins of the Church. The Irish government set up a Commission of Inquiry to look into child sexual and physical abuse in our country and to find out the reasons why child abuse was so rampant and widespread in state and semi-state institutions and industrial Christian Brothers schools such as Letterfrack in the west of Ireland, and the most famous of them all, Artane Christian Brothers Boys Industrial School.

Once the Commission of Enquiry into Child Sex Abuse in State and Semi-state Run Institutions and Convents was set up by the government, the Commission was given several very important functions: it would, of course, examine the reasons why child abuse was so widespread.

It would also allow survivors of child sexual-physical abuse to give their own account to the Commission of Inquiry in a very safe environment where their stories would be fully investigated; so it would eventually formulate guidelines that would help protect children against any recurrence of those awful situations where such abuse could flourish. The Irish government, led by Bertie Ahern, was determined that no child should suffer in this way ever again. They gave the Commission widespread powers. They appointed a high court judge, Justice Mary Laffoy, to be chairperson of the Commission.

The abuse of young children in state-funded organisations and religious boarding schools was not unique to Ireland. Therefore the government decided to look at the situation in other countries.

One such example was to be found in Newfoundland in Canada where, in 1989, a Royal Commission of Enquiry was set up to investigate Mount Cashel, an orphanage. Mount Cashel was in fact run by the Order of the Irish Christian Brothers, which had allowed a couple of proven child sex abusers to leave the province to go to a Catholic-run treatment centre without ever having to face criminal charges.

The Commission discovered a whole generation of boys scarred by sexual abuse at the hands of people entrusted with protecting them. The hearings of the Commission in Newfoundland were held in public, many of which were broadcast live on TV and radio. A huge number of victims gave their accounts of the horrendous abuse and indignities they suffered as young boys at the hands of the Christian Brothers. The people were shocked by this!

The Commission gave the Christian Brothers every opportunity to testify and defend themselves against such evil accusations, but they refused. Before the end of 1990 well over 150 charges were brought against the Order of the Christian Brothers by the Commission as a result of their investigation into Mount Cashel.

Many other countries set up enquiries into child abuse. In Queensland, Australia in 1998, the Commission investigated reported child abuse in over 100 orphanages and detention centres dating back over eighty years.

The Commission found that many religious state-funded institutions failed to provide for the very basic human needs of the children in their care. In my case I found it awfully difficult to come to terms with having to face up to my bleak past in Artane Industrial School from 1950.

Once I had agreed to cooperate and state my complete case to the detectives appointed to investigate cases of child abuse,

I realised I had to travel far back along that terrible bleak road to Artane Industrial Christian Brothers School of the early 1950s. It struck me hard when I had to reveal the kind of abuse kids such as me suffered during those fearful nights in the dormitories. I wept openly in front of the hardened detectives and my lawyers as I described those awful events.

I lay awake at night so often listening to kids crying for help, crying in pain after a fierce beating across their naked buttocks for some very minor offence, many crying out, calling for their mums and dads, all in vain. Though they were the lucky ones I felt, as many like me had no one to turn to for help.

I had promised Pauline that I'd cooperate fully with the detectives and my solicitors in giving a full account of the details of abuse I suffered. I really felt at the time it would be no problem; however, in reality, it was far different than I ever envisaged. I was confident within myself that I could answer all the questions put to me by the team and I'd simply shake their hands, enjoy a cup of coffee with them and go home. Reality is so different to dreams of what one may think or wish to think, the way such things pan out. In fact, I had a prepared script for the event, notes of dates, times, names, etc.

When the hardened young detective faced me across the long polished mahogany table, his smile vanished as did mine with his first question, for which I was unprepared. 'So why did you not describe all the abuse you suffered in your book *Fear of the Collar* in 1990?'

'Well,' I began, 'I was not an experienced writer and though I did write on sexual abuse for the book, at the time I found it most difficult to write about, almost impossible in fact. However, I did submit some scripts for the book; but my publishers felt strongly that the country was ill-prepared for such revelations as child sex abuse and physical sex abuse in 1990. A time would come when all the true facts would be revealed, they believed.'

My lawyers were in full agreement, as were the team of detectives, with my answers. It was far from being an easy ride. It was awful having to travel back to those awful events of my past. I felt more than ever that the shadow of Artane had never gone away.

The team of specially appointed detectives took several years to compile over 7,000 statements. As my own case began to take shape I was relieved to be over the most difficult part in giving my statement to the detectives and to my lawyers who were incredibly helpful to me. I am most grateful to my solicitors Lavelle Coleman, and the team of detectives assigned to the case, for the superb job they've done in helping to bring closure for the thousands of victims of child abuse in Ireland's bleak past.

I heard nothing regarding my case for some time; however, an appointment was made for me to visit a psychiatrist. Once again I found myself reliving my extraordinary childhood in Artane Industrial Christian Brothers School and, though the lady doctor was most sympathetic, I found the whole experience harrowing and very emotional.

It was of great relief to me to get out on Saturdays and Sundays as a soccer referee and put the whole of my dark, bleak, childhood past in Artane Industrial School behind me. For those few hours all thoughts of Artane School would vanish from my mind and I often wished it could remain that way.

The fact that I was taking official control of a sport that we were strictly forbidden to participate in inside Artane was rarely ever lost on me, as I'd stand in the centre circle before kick-off, I'd glance across to my children and some of their school pals and smile with the satisfying thought that at least they are now free to choose whatever sport they wish to participate in.

It took until 2002 for my own case to reach a satisfying conclusion, over fifty years since I was sent to Artane.

I wish to pay tribute to the survivors of child abuse, over 7,000 of whom had the harrowing experience of reliving their childhood memories of that awful bleak time in Ireland, an Ireland without a breath of warmth or love for so many in need as I was. Although the Christian Brothers had marked me for life, they had no part whatsoever in my being sent to Artane. An uncaring, selfish judge had done that because, as he said in court that morning in Kilmainham, 'I have no place else to send you.' With those words he sent me to eight years of hard labour and fear, eight years that defined the rest of my life.

However badly I was treated, I tried my hardest to treat others well. Despite my upbringing, I became a successful baker, a well-travelled man, a published author, a husband to Pauline, and proud father to my three beautiful children, Paula, John and Suzanne. And I have tried, despite the shackles of my past, to live as free as I could, as free as a bird.

Epilogue

May Brennan once told me that November is the month of the fallen leaf, and throughout my life I have had cause to reflect on her words. Some of the most difficult events of my life have fallen within that month – I was first sexually abused by the Macker in November; I became deathly ill with a perforated ulcer in November, and in November 1999 I buried my beautiful wife, Pauline.

But November 2007 was different in every way. This November was a month of happiness, pride and hope for the future. As the hard rain fell and the autumn winds blew, I was looking forward to the day ahead with joy in my heart. On this day I would be walking my eldest child, Paula, down the aisle.

After Pauline died it was as if time stood still. On the day after she was laid to rest, I was home, by myself. There were her clothes, her shoes, her make-up; there were the photos that hung on the walls in which she smiled her lovely, radiant smile, but her beautiful presence was gone. A few weeks after

I lost Pauline, I stood staring across the sea from the cliffs at Hampton Cove when I was struck by a strange thought, 'tis death that brings us home to our final dwelling place.

Suzanne had decided to stay with Sylvie's family for a while, because it was difficult for her to be in the house without her mum in it. And so I was alone, in this house that was no longer a home, without the warmth a wife and children brought to it.

What helped me during that sad, lonely and difficult time were the words of Bishop O'Mahony and Father Carey as they stood in the front room. 'Remember how strong Pauline was in her desperate fight to live. Remember how she smiled the whole way through her awful illness. Be strong for her, Pat, have hope, and pray to God and to Pauline for guidance and help and strength to get through.'

I haven't ever stopped praying to Pauline, and it brings me an enormous amount of comfort.

I spent the millennium celebrations with Pauline's brothers Jim and Tony, and Tony's wife, Delores, and it was a difficult time for all of us. But however dark days are, life goes on; and slowly, as winter faded into spring and the days grew lighter, so too did my mood. The Commission of Enquiry into Child Abuse was up and running, and although that was bringing back some terrible memories for me, I was beginning to feel that what had been done to generations of children was finally being addressed and acknowledged by the government, and the Catholic church.

By spring Suzanne had moved back home, and after school would bring her friends home with her. The rooms were filled with laughter once more as their young voices filled the house. I realised I'd have to find work to support myself and Suzanne as she was studying for her final exams, hoping to gain enough points to get her a place in university in the autumn.

In April 2000, I was offered a temporary job as a porter in a bank in the city. I couldn't quite believe it! Instead of my normal baking kit, a well-tailored suit, tie and shirts came with the position. I would start each morning with a leisurely breakfast while I listened to the radio, get ready, and leave for work at the respectable time of 8am – during my baking days I would have been working for five hours by then!

Suzanne won her place in the University of Ulster in Coleraine. She was thrilled. I was so proud of her, and so relieved I was working. I couldn't ever recall a time in my life when everything quite simply fell into place – and it would have been perfect if only Pauline had been there to see her daughter start university. But now I was by myself for good, apart from the times Paula, John or Suzanne would come to visit.

My job in the bank was coming to an end, and I worried that I would have to go back to baking. I really didn't want to do that. I had grown used to the hours, and dreaded the thought of going back to my old life. I applied for an office job in the post room of an insurance brokers' firm, and was over the moon when I got the position. If change is as good as a rest then it had the opposite effect on me. I soon realised how little I knew, being computer illiterate was a huge draw-back. However, I toughed it out and I learned a great deal, gaining invaluable experience and knowledge from so many wise and very mature people there. It was a job I held until my retirement in December 2007.

It hasn't all been plain sailing. On holiday in Malta in September 2002, I began to be troubled by weakness and shortness of breath. To walk any distance was a great struggle for me. After an extremely bad night, during which I was rushed to the hospital, I was told that I had severe blockage of my main arteries and would need a heart bypass within six months. I stayed in hospital in Malta for months while I built up enough strength to be moved to a hospital in Ireland.

Finally I was given the all-clear to return home on the condition it was by air ambulance. I was released from the hospital to a nursing home where I remained for a few weeks until the arrangements were made. Finally the day came to leave Malta. I boarded a small Cesna air ambulance with just one other male patient, a doctor and a nurse. The plane landed in France for refuelling and I was allowed to get off to enjoy some fresh air and coffee. But slowly I began to feel the strain, and pain and tension crept up upon me.

The next part of the journey was to Manchester. The flight seemed to take all day. Perhaps it did. When we had another refuelling stop at Manchester I felt so bad my legs went from under me. I woke up in the cardiac care unit in Wythenshawe Hospital, Manchester.

An English nurse was standing by my bedside. Her smile was soft and filled with warmth. The doctor who came with me from Malta assured me I was in the best place. He kindly explained everything to me – I was to be kept here in Manchester for a few weeks to be fully checked out. He asked me for Paula's number – she would be waiting for me at the airport – and called her using his mobile phone. He passed the phone down to me. 'Take your time.'

Hearing Paula's voice made me feel better. It raised me up as she quickly explained how they were all so anxious to come over and see me in Manchester. 'I promise you, Dad, we will all get over. In fact, I can't wait, Dad, I promise you we will come over as soon as we can. I promise you, Dad, love always, bye.' It was a promise she faithfully kept.

I will always remember being wheeled into the operating theatre on 12 November 2002. I'd heard so much about how run down the British health system was. Not a day went by without the National Health Service being held up to ridicule on TV and in the newspapers. Yet here was I, lying in a state-of-the-art operating theatre undergoing life-saving surgery. I prayed to Pauline for strength and help to get me safely through it.

After the angioplasty the cardiologist came by my bedside and confirmed to me the wonderful news that the surgery was a complete success. My prayers had been answered.

I left the South Manchester Wythenshawe Hospital in late November 2002. I am extremely grateful for the wonderful treatment and care given to me by the doctors, nurses and staff at the hospital and, in particular, for the fantastic treatment I received from the cardiac team and the consultant cardiologist there. As a result I have been able to live and work, and lead an active normal life ever since. I have been given a second chance.

There are times when I can't help but wonder how differently my life would have been if I hadn't been sent away to Artane at the age of eight. My life in Barnacullia had been idyllic; I was happy and healthy doing my chores and playing in the fresh air with my friend, Shep the dog. Bridget Doyle looked after me, and loved me, and I was safe and secure in the warmth of her home. There wasn't much money to go around, but I was well fed on good food, school was a place of learning and my sleep was filled with good dreams, not the nightmares that would come to plague me in my later years.

Artane was the complete opposite of my life until then. I was sometimes abused, often hungry and always scared. I developed nightmares and would walk in my sleep. Christian Brothers that were charged with looking after us in fact tormented and sexually abused us. We orphans, with no family to worry about us, were placed there by the state, forgotten about by society and used at the Christian Brothers' pleasure. And we were denied the one thing that could have improved our later lives immeasurably: education.

But if I had stayed in Barnacullia, content and happy, would I ever have had the drive to travel, to see and live in exotic countries? Possibly not, and I would have missed out on some of the most enriching experiences of my life. Would I have met Pauline and brought up my three wonderful children? Chances are, my path never would have crossed with Pauline's, and that is unthinkable. And I would never have had the urge to write, and to tell my story. The fact is, you have to make the most out of what you have been given, and while Artane may have broken my body and cowed my spirit, it also instilled within me a drive to succeed, as a baker, a family man and a writer.

Artane may have marked me, it may have shaped me, but I made myself the man I am today. I have confronted the demons of my past and I have made peace with them. It has been a long, tough road – over fifty years long – and I am a different person to that poor, institutionalised boy who left

Artane, terrified of the world outside its walls. And Ireland is different too; I hope that no other generation of children will be forgotten about, suffering and living in fear as I and my mates did, so many years ago.

It is 17 November 2007, a typical autumn day, wild with rain and blustery with wind. Today, though, is not a day for looking back at the past: today is filled with hope for the future. I am with my daughter Paula, and we are outside the beautiful grey, sandstone church of St Peter's and Paul's in Balbriggan. The church bells are pealing, announcing the arrival of the bride. Paula is as beautiful and as radiant as her mother was on our wedding day, and my heart swells with pride as I take her arm in mine and we enter the church.

Everyone's faces turn towards us as we enter. There is Alan Ryan, Paula's fiancé, soon-to-be husband, waiting for her at the end. I see my son, John, and his beautiful girlfriend, Margarita Gormes, on the bride's side of the church. My son John is easy going, very honest. He is sincere and very hard working. They're looking after Paula's baby son Cameron, my first grandson. And there beside them is Suzanne, my youngest, with the man she is soon to marry, Phil Waring, smiling and looking so happy for her sister. She's a teacher, now. My family, here in this church, celebrating the marriage of my eldest child: there is no happier or prouder man on earth than I at this moment.

I give my daughter away, and step back to observe the rest of the proceedings. I feel Pauline's presence beside me. November is the month in which she died, and it is the month that holds my darkest memories, but my youngest was born in November, and now there is another happy memory to add – my eldest daughter's wedding.

On this wild and wet but beautifully glorious November day, the shadow that Artane cast over my life has all but disappeared. I will always have the scars, but they have long since healed, and are finally beginning to fade.

With my children (from left to right): Suzanne, Paula and John